Journal of Research
of the
American Federation
of Astrologers

Volume 14

Copyright 2014 by American Federation of Astrologers, Inc.

No part of this book may be reproduced or transcribed in any form or by any means, electronic or mechanical, including photocopying or recording or by any information storage and retrieval system without written permission from the author and publisher, except in the case of brief quotations embodied in critical reviews and articles. Requests and inquiries may be mailed to: American Federation of Astrologers, Inc., 6535 S. Rural Road, Tempe, AZ 85283.

ISBN-10: 0-86690-648-7
ISBN-13: 978-0-86690-648-7

Cover Design: Jack Cipolla

Published by:
American Federation of Astrologers, Inc.
6535 S. Rural Road
Tempe, AZ 85283

www.astrologers.com

Printed in the United States of America

In Memory of
James H. Holden, 1926-2013
AFA Director of Research, 1982-2013

Contents

An Astrological Theory of Personality By James H. Holden, FAFA	7
An Economic Comparison of the 1930s and 2000s By Kris Brandt Riske, PMAFA	13
Planetary Arc Directions By Stephanie Jean Clement Ph.D., FAFA	23
An Astrological Perspective on Women's Rights Issues By Marilyn J. Muir LPMAFA	49
The Child and the Marriage Chart By DaCosta E. Williams, FAFA	59
The Autopsy of an Election By Marilyn J. Muir, LPMAFA	65
Women's Astrology in India By Ronnie Gale Dreyer, MAFA	79
Predicting Events By Chand Karan Ahuja, RMAFA	99
Asteroids Strong (or Weak) by Midpoint–Juno By Michael Munkasey, PMAFA	111

An Astrological Theory of Personality

By James H. Holden, FAFA

Three factors in the horoscope are of fundamental importance. Everything else modifies their significations but does not basically alter them.

The Ascendant represents the physical body of the native, including his nervous system. It thus indicates what we might call the "animal nature" of the individual. It is automatic and unthinking. It shows how an individual will act or react without any conscious direction from the mind. As an analogy, consider the natural difference in behavior of a cat and a rabbit. If you throw something in front of a cat, it will pounce upon it. But if you throw the same thing in front of a rabbit, it will run away. This is instinctive behavior, and that is what the Ascendant indicates.

The Moon represents the conscious mind. It is independent of the Ascendant, and it is independent of the Sun.

The Sun represents a sort of internal standard of what seems to be right and what seems to be wrong. In a limited sense it represents the native's ethical standard; it is not a learned standard, but rather an innate one. It is independent of the Moon and independent of the Ascendant.

The primary astrological influence on each of these three factors is the zodiacal sign in which it is placed. Thus, there are 12 X 12 X 12 = 1,728 possible combinations. These are the basic personality types. But each sign is modified if it also contains one or more planets; hence, the actual number of possible variations of these 1,728 combinations is much greater.

Of the five possible combinations of the three signs, the most common is the one in which each of the three factors is in a different sign. There are 12 X 11 X 10 = 1,320 of these. This combination includes roughly three-fourths of humanity. And these people represent a rather muddled mixture of the three factors. They think one way, they judge correctness in another way, and they instinctively act in a third way. They have internal mental conflicts, and they are sometimes dissatisfied with their actions for one of four reasons: 1) they did something instinctively that they did not want to do; 2) they did something that they did want to do, but they feel that they should not have wanted to do it; 3) they did something that they didn't really want to do, but they felt that it was the "right" thing to do; or, 4) they did something either because they wanted to do it or because they thought they ought to do it, but they had to force themselves to do it because it went against their instinctive nature. Some of their excuses are: "I don't know why I did that." "I really shouldn't have done that, but I did it anyway." "It wasn't what I wanted to do, but I thought it was the right thing to do, so I did it." "I wanted to do it, although I didn't think it was right, but I did it as best I could." "I wanted to do it, and I thought it was the right thing to do, but I had to force myself to do it."

If the Moon and the Sun are in the same sign, but the Ascendant is in a different sign, then the individual's thoughts generally harmonize with his internal standard. Whatever he thinks is judged to be appropriate. There is no internal conflict in his thinking, although there may be difficulty in taking action, or his action may be altered somewhat from his intention–"I did it, but I had to force myself." "I did it, but I didn't do it as well as

I would have liked to do it." There are 12 X 11 = 132 of these types.

If the Moon and the Ascendant are in the same sign, but the Sun is in a different sign, then the individual's thoughts harmonize with his instinctive nature, but his internal standard may disapprove. Whatever he thinks, he may do without any physical conflict, but he may feel that his action is inappropriate–"I did it just as I had in mind to do it, but I probably shouldn't have done it." There are 12 X 11 = 132 of these types.

If the Sun and the Ascendant are in the same sign, but the Moon is in a different sign, then the individual's thoughts do not harmonize with his internal standard and his instinctive nature. He may wish to do something and immediately think that it would be inappropriate to do it and that he would have difficulty doing it; but whatever he finally decides to do, he does without any physical conflict and without any feeling of impropriety, but he may be intellectually dissatisfied with having done it. He may also feel at times that he is acting in a manner that is appropriate but that is different from the manner in which he would like to act. There are 12 X 11 = 132 of these types. One occupational example would be an actor who plays a particular role well, and is satisfied with his performance, but who does not think like the character he portrays

If all three factors–Ascendant, Moon, and Sun–are in the same sign, there is no internal conflict and no dissatisfaction with actions. Whatever the individual decides to do, he does (circumstances permitting), and he is satisfied with the intent, the appropriateness, and the quality of his action. There are only 12 of these types. They are the rare "triples."

The Moon and the Sun acting in combination determine the internal thinking and decision-making process within an individual. The Moon has a thought; this is judged by the standard set by the Sun. It may be approved or disapproved. It may be retained or rejected. If the thought is retained and it requires physical action, then it must act through the Ascendant. The nature of the Ascendant affects the manifestation of the thought, although it can be deliberately overridden to some extent by the Moon. In other words, an individual may choose to do something that is contrary to the nature of his Ascendant. This is commonly called "forcing himself to do something." For example, a man with the Moon in Aries may decide to take some bold and physically hazardous action that his Pisces Ascendant instinctively shrinks from, but he may force himself to do it anyway (perhaps while shaking with fear).

A planet in the same sign with one of these three factors alters its action in accordance with the nature of the planet. For example, Mars in the Ascendant sign makes the individual bolder and more forceful in instinctive action than he would otherwise be. Mars in the Moon sign makes the individual bolder and more forceful in thought. He may think that forceful action is required (but he may not take such action). Mars in the Sun sign makes bold and forceful action seem appropriate.

If the Ascendant is stronger (by sign or by planetary influence) than the Moon or the Sun, then instinct predominates. The individual may take actions on the spur of the moment that he subsequently wishes he hadn't taken or that he thinks were inappropriate.

If the Moon is stronger than the Ascendant or the Sun, then thought predominates. The individual may think many things, but he may not do them, either because they go against his instinctive nature or because they are judged to be inappropriate.

If the Sun is stronger than the Ascendant or the Moon, then the individual's internal standard predominates, and he may think or instinctively desire to do many things, but he restrains himself; or if he does act, he acts more in accordance with his internal standard than with his instinctive nature or with his thoughts.

The ancients judged a person by his Moon sign, the moderns

by his Sun sign, but some astrologers (notably, Englishman Vivian Robson) more by his Ascendant. Robson says if he had to give up all the astrological factors but one, he would keep the Ascendant. This means that he judged that people acted more in accordance with their instincts than with their thoughts or their internal standards of right and wrong.

Other factors in the horoscope, such as aspects and house positions, are significant. But I have found that the basic personality is accurately described by the factors mentioned above.

In meeting a person for the first time, we are immediately impressed by his Ascendant, but after we get to know him, we may judge him according to his Moon sign or Sun sign (or the combination of the two). This is also the explanation of why we sometimes say later, "I like his looks, but I don't like his actions." Or the other way around. As mentioned above, most people are influenced by three signs, so we can understand that their outward appearance and mannerisms (Ascendant) may be at odds with their thoughts (Moon) or with their internal standards (Sun), which we can only come to know with acquaintance.

However, there are times when the Ascendant works by itself. If a person drinks enough alcohol, the Moon and the Sun are somehow blocked out, and the person then behaves solely in accordance with his Ascendant. This may cause him to act totally differently from his normal behavior. Hence we may see him displaying the condition known as "the happy drunk" or "the mean drunk." I once knew a man who was ordinarily very calm and mild mannered; but on the rare occasions when he got drunk, he would become very aggressive and would challenge everyone he met "to fight." This would seem to indicate that the Sun and the Moon influence the portion of the personality that resides in the brain; but the Ascendant represents the portion that resides in the entire body's muscular and nervous system.

An Economic Comparison of the 1930s and 2000s

By Kris Brandt Riske, PMAFA

The United States has experienced a number of economic downturns–recessions and depressions–throughout its history. Yet none is so striking as the 1930s, the decade known as the Great Depression. The current economic crisis, known as the Great Recession (and also described as the Little Depression) mirrors the Great Depression in many ways. The two periods have much in common, both from an economic perspective and an astrological one. There are key differences, however, some of which are the result of programs established during the Great Depression.

Definitions

The National Bureau of Economic Research (NBER) defines a recession as "a significant decline in economic activity spread across the economy, lasting more than a few months, normally visible in real gross domestic product, real income, employment, industrial production, and wholesale-retail sales." There have been nearly fifty recessions in American history, although some of these are open to interpretation because of the lack of nationwide records regarding employment, income, production, etc.

A depression can be defined as a long-term recession (some economists define this as two or more years) in which unemployment figures are extremely high, credit availability and production are low, bankruptcies and bank failures are high, and wholesale-retail sales are significanrly reduced. It is often preceded by a widespread financial crisis. Whether economists are reluctant to use the word "depression," particularly since the end of World War II, these economic cycles may have occurred more often than the two generally recognized periods: the 1870s (including the Panic of 1873) and the 1930s. NBER does not declare depressions.

The recession/depression cycle, which is a normal economic cycle, can be simply defined as financial expansion followed by financial contraction. Credit is easy in the years leading up to the economic downturn, employment is high, and prices and availability of goods and housing rise. The pattern reverses during the contraction phase of the cycle. This can be likened to a chain of dominoes; when the first one falls, it triggers the rest of the dominoes in the chain until all economic factors are involved.

In both the 1920s and 2000s, the first domino fell when housing prices and construction began to decline. People were laid off and no longer had the funds to buy goods or repay debt, followed by a resulting decline in industrial production and more layoffs, followed by bankruptcies and foreclosures, bank failures, and lack of the credit necessary to reverse the cycle.

Those not substantially and directly affected by the downturn (i.e., those who are employed and paying their debts) are nevertheless a component of the cycle because they generally designate a higher percentage of their income to pay down debt and increase savings. (The savings rate between 1929 and 1931 was 97.5 percent higher than average between 1926 and 1928. In 2008, the savings rate rose to 8.3 percent, with a gradual decline to about 3.6 percent in 2012.)

Housing

Although the stock market crash of October 1929 is commonly viewed as the event that triggered the Great Depression, the cycle that led to what was arguably the worst decade in American history began in 1925-26 with a decline in housing prices and construction. This had of course been preceded by the housing boom that began in 1921-22, following the post-World War I trough. Housing prices fell moderately for about two years prior to a sharp decline and collapse between 1929 and 1931; the housing market bottomed in 1934. As prices fell, fewer homes were built (housing starts declined 40.4 percent between 1925 and 1929), and fewer changed hands because people did not have enough equity in their homes. Interest-only mortgages and those with balloon payments were popular at the time, and underwriting standards were weak. Credit continued to expand through 1929, which was partly responsible for the stock market crash.

Mortgage lending had increased in the early 1920s, when installment credit also became popular as people filled their homes with everything from radios to furnishings to appliances. Auto manufacturers also benefitted from the boom, but sales began to fall in 1926, dropping from 10.3 percent per year in 1926 to 5.3 percent per year in 1929. It was a time of high consumption, low unemployment, and high industrial production that would end at the onset of the Great Depression.

Astrologically, real estate and business are associated with Saturn, and money with Jupiter and Pluto. The Saturn-Pluto square of 1922, along with the Uranus-Pluto trine of 1921 and 1922 signaled the end of the post-war recession. In 1925, 1926, and 1927 (twice), Saturn was trine Uranus (change), which would signal a change for the better in housing prices. But Saturn and Neptune formed a square three times in 1926, an aspect that indicated the bursting housing bubble (Neptune). Once the Saturn-Uranus trine made its last aspect in 1927, there were no longer any positive astrological influences for the housing market. During these years, Jupiter (expansion) was in Scorpio (money) in 1922-23; in upbeat, expansive Sagittarius in 1923-24; in Capricorn (contraction) in 1924-25; and in Aquarius (ruled by Saturn and Uranus) in 1926-27.

After the 1929 stock market crash, astrological aspects reflect the continued downtrend of housing. Saturn formed a square with Uranus five times in 1930-31, along with three Uranus-Pluto oppositions in 1931.

After the dot-com recession of the early 2000s, the economy stabilized and housing prices and construction began to rise. They peaked in 2005-06, prior to which easy credit was the norm with people again taking out interest-only mortgages and lenders using "stated" income rather than requiring proof. At the same time, people used their homes as ATMs, taking out home equity loans to finance improvements, vehicles, furnishings, trips, and big-screen TVs–almost anything a homeowner could desire could be funded. Underwriting standards were weak, as they were in the 1920s. Housing starts declined 43.9 percent between 2006 and 2007.

Jupiter was in Libra, Scorpio, and Sagittarius as housing prices peaked, just as it was in the 1920s, and in Capricorn in 2008, as prices began to decline.

Housing prices bottomed in late 2009/early 2010, with the Case Shiller National Housing Price Index showing a drop in prices of 35.5 percent between 2006 and 2011. Twenty-two percent of mortgages had less equity than the outstanding mortgage balance in 2012.

Here, too, the astrological aspects reflect the cycle of boom and bust. The Saturn-Uranus square of 2000 and the Saturn-Pluto opposition of 2002 were replaced with a Saturn-Uranus trine in 2002-03. In 2006 and 2007, there were three Saturn-Neptune oppositions, along with a Saturn-Pluto trine in 2007. Saturn formed a series of oppositions with Uranus between

2008 and 2010, the years during which housing prices fell and bottomed.

From an astrological perspective, the aspects during the Great Depression related to housing were more severe, if only from the standpoint that they were in effect for many more years than the aspects of the Great Recession. The overall economy, however, has yet to completely recover from the Great Recession, despite increasingly positive indicators that are largely the result of the actions of the Federal Reserve and social entitlement programs that were not in place during the 1930s.

Aspect Comparison for Housing

1921-22 Uranus trine Pluto	2000 Saturn square Uranus
1922 Saturn square Pluto	2002 Saturn opposition Pluto
1925, 1926, 1927 Saturn trine Uranus	2002-03 Saturn trine Uranus
1926 Saturn square Neptune	2006-07 Saturn opposition Neptune
1930-31 Saturn square Uranus	2008-10 Saturn opposition Uranus
1931 Saturn opposition Pluto	

Stock Market

The combination of easy credit and few financial regulations triggered the October-November 1929 market crash. At the time many people purchased equities on margin, with an upfront investment of only ten percent. The rising market fueled speculation, much as the rising housing market did in the 2000s, when some people acquired 100 percent mortgages. The belief was that the market, like real estate prices many years later, could only go up.

The bull market of the 1920s lasted nine years, with the Dow Jones Industrial Average rising tenfold to 381.17 on September 3, 1929, followed by days of volatility and high volume. October 24 brought the first steep decline, with the market falling eleven percent at the opening bell amid heavy trading. The day ended with the market down only about six percent because of large purchases by a number of bankers in an attempt to stabilize the market. This was not enough to restore confidence, however, as the market fell thirteen percent on October 28, and another twelve percent the following day, despite yet another attempt by bankers to stabilize the market. The heavy volume of October 29 set a record that would not be broken for forty years, and the market would not again reach the September 3, 1929 high until November 23, 1954.

Prior to the Great Recession the market rose throughout much of 2007, but dropped in 2008 as the government initiated bailouts for Bear Stearns, Fannie Mae, Freddie Mac, AIG, and the auto industry, and as unemployment figures increased. From a May high of more than 13,000, the market ended the year at 8776.39, down thirty-four percent. A new high was reached on July 24, 2009, at 9093.24, and the market has been in an overall uptrend since then.

1929 was characterized by a Saturn-Neptune trine, which occurred in March, May, and December, followed by five Saturn-Uranus squares in 1930-31. During the Great Recession, the market bottomed in 2008 under a Saturn-Uranus opposition, and reached a new high in 2013 under a Saturn-Pluto sextile and a Saturn-Neptune trine.

Unemployment

Unemployment rates rise during a recession or depression, which is perhaps the most apparent effect of an economic downturn. When industrial production falls, unemployment rises, causing production and employment to fall yet again in a downward spiral. This in turn leads to diminished spending power, bankruptcy, and home foreclosure, all of which keep the negative cycle active, sometimes for many years, as during the decade of the 1930s.

By any measurement, unemployment levels during the Great Depression were much more severe than those of the Great Recession. Unemployment reached a high of twenty-five percent in 1933, and had only fallen to seventeen percent by 1939. During the Great Recession, unemployment peaked in late 2009/early 2010 at ten percent, "recovering" about six months after the stock market. However, the U6 unemployment rate (what some refer to as the "real" unemployment rate because it includes those who are underemployed or have stopped searching for work) was seventeen percent.

The Saturn-Pluto square and Saturn-Uranus opposition of 2009-10 are thus associated with the unemployment rate of the Great Recession. The Saturn-Uranus square of 1930-31, the Saturn-Pluto opposition of 1931 during the Great Depression reflect rising unemployment, and it wasn't until the passing of the Saturn-Pluto square that unemployment levels declined significantly, mostly as a result of increased military spending prior to World War II. Prior to that there was movement to the positive under the Saturn-Pluto trine of 1937-38.

Banks

Bank failures were another significant factor of the Great Depression, a trend that began in earnest with the failure of the Bank of the United States in late 1930. Eventually about 9,000 banks failed during the 1930s, a trend that was aggravated by the small size of many and the level of lending vs. deposits. At the time most banks were small institutions located in smaller and rural communities, with a bank's lending levels directly tied to its deposits.

The bank runs of the early 1930s depleted deposits, and in many cases there were insufficient funds to pay the depositors. As the Great Depression deepened, more banks failed when homeowners and farmers could not make their mortgage and other loan payments. Foreclosures reached a peak in 1932-33, exceeding one percent, with as many as 1,000 properties placed in foreclosure every day in 1933. By contrast, foreclosure rates during the Great Recession are estimated at two percent of all properties.

Banks also failed during the Great Recession, although not at the rate of the 1930s. Unlike the fifty percent rate of the Great Depression, the rate is less than one percent for the Great Recession. This is mostly because of the Federal Deposit Insurance Corporation (FDIC), which was established on June 16, 1933 as a result of the 1930s banking crisis. In most cases the FDIC was able to arrange for another bank to acquire a failing one. Most deposits were also insured by the FDIC.

The majority of the 1930s failures occurred under a Saturn-Uranus square and a Saturn-Pluto opposition. During the Great Recession, the aspects were a Saturn-Uranus opposition and a Saturn-Pluto square.

Recovery

The Uranus-Pluto square of 1932-33 is often cited as *the* aspect of the Great Depression. As much as it characterizes continuing unemployment and a dire economy, it likely has more to do with recovery than crisis. This also appears to be true of the same planetary alignment during the Great Recession.

However, there are significant differences between then and now. The early and mid 1930s saw the establishment of social entitlement programs such as unemployment insurance and Social Security, along with significant reform in and establishment of banking and securities regulations. All of these represented change (Uranus) at the deepest financial level (Pluto). Never before had the government been the last resort in periods of economic crisis, at least not to this extent. The same years saw the passage of other legislation that funded the Civilian Conservation Corps, the Works Project Administration, and many similar programs, as well as an increasing federal deficit. Government expanded at an exponential rate, creating the foundation for massive and ever-growing bureaucracy that is the norm today.

Also of importance, although much debated by economists and politicians, is the effect of actions by the Federal Reserve. during the Great Depression the money supply was increased by seventeen percent only in one year, 1933; since 2007, the Federal Reserve has infused the economy with tens of billions of dollars and continues to do so seven years later. This move seems to have eased the recovery, but only time will reveal the outcome. Ben Bernanke, Federal Reserve chairman during most of these years and a student of the Great Depression, pushed for the Federal Reserve to take action during the Great Recession.

A Uranus-Pluto square is again active, as it was during the Great Depression, with two exact contacts in each year from 2012 to 2014 and a final contact in 2015. The deficit is, predictably, a topic of Great Recession conversation, as are some of the entitlement programs established in the 1930s. No citizen wants to give up what has now become the norm and return to the country without entitlements that existed prior to the 1930s. There is no question that banking and securities regulations will undergo further changes between 2012 and 2015, as will entitlements. The process this time, however, will be longer and more difficult, given the length of the Uranus-Pluto square–two years during the Great Depression and four years during the Great Recession.

Resources

Egan, Timothy, *The Worst Hard Time*, Mariner Books, 2007.

Gjerstad, Steven and Smith, Vernon L., "Consumption and Investment Booms in the Twenties and Their Collapse in 1930," National Bureau of Economic Research, 2012.

Parker, Randall, "An Overview of the Great Depression," East Carolina University, 2005.

Watkins, T. H., *The Great Depression: America in the 1930s*, Back Bay Books, 2009.

Planetary Arc Directions

By Stephanie Jean Clement Ph.D., FAFA

This paper aims to achieve three specific goals:
to test the Sibley chart for the U.S.
- to demonstrate the use and efficacy of planetary arc directed charts, and
- to accomplish the above goals using charts for events in U.S. history.

Having studied thousands of charts for individuals, organizations and nations, I am tired of charts for disasters, illness, death, accident, unemployment, and heartbreak of all kinds. Even though those topics comprise the bulk of work for many astrologers, it is not all there is to our science and art.

I have chosen to examine charts for people and events that I feel represent a more optimistic side of life—positive, creative, constructive, dynamic, far-reaching, and yes, spiritually inspiring possibilities that are outgrowths of admittedly less fortunate events in some cases.

For the purpose of fulfilling the first goal, I have chosen to examine the Sibley chart for the U.S., and to contrast its time of 5:10 pm with a slightly later time—5:24:30 pm (a time suggested by Jeffrey Sayer Close). I have also included personal birth charts for Lyndon B. Johnson and Neil Armstrong.

A theme emerges in the data I have selected:

> "We hold these truths to be self-evident, that all men are created equal, that they are endowed by their creator with certain inalienable rights. . . ."–*Declaration of Independence*

> "Four score and seven years ago our fathers brought forth on this continent a new nation conceived in liberty, and dedicated to the proposition that all men are created equal."–*Gettysburg Address*

> "One hundred and eighty-eight years ago this week a small band of valiant men began a long struggle for freedom. They pledged their lives . . . to forge an ideal of freedom. . . . Now our generation of Americans has been called on to continue the unending search for justice within our own borders."–*Johnson at signing of the Civil Rights Act of 1964*

> "One small step for [a] man, one giant step for mankind."–*Neil Armstrong from the surface of the Moon*

To accomplish the second goal, this article considers planetary arc directions. As with solar arc directions, planetary arcs are symbolic movements of the entire chart wheel, either forward or converse in direction from the birth date at the rate of one day per year. This technique provides a timing device of extraordinary accuracy. What level of precision are we talking about? I am looking at aspects within 15' of arc or less.

I believe one of astrology's strengths is the capacity to accurately forecast future situations and conditions. We can identify periods of time of great stress, creativity, or potential success and thereby help people to choose better times for specific activities. On April 14, 1865, Abraham Lincoln went out with his wife to attend a play. With a bit of astrological guidance, he might have found other uses for his time and avoided assassination.

Other people, including John and Robert Kennedy, Martin Luther King, Jr., and Ronald Reagan might have found themselves in different places, doing different things, on crucial dates. But those are not the examples I will use in this article. I have considered a few milestones in U.S. history relating to civil rights.

Background of the Planetary Arc Technique

Solar, Lunar and Planetary Arc Directions

Acknowledging a wealth of other predictive methods, Reinhold Ebertin mentioned that "Many kinds of directions have been invented in the course of time. We will concern ourselves with those directions that are most easily understandable and that can be substantiated." (p. 15 *Directions*). Referencing the *Bible*, Ebertin goes on to say that the Sun travels about one degree of the zodiac in one day, and one day equals one year of life.

A major difference between arc directions—solar, lunar, or planetary—and other progression methods is the fact that the entire wheel moves at the rate of the designated planet in directed charts. We are most familiar with the solar arc, which varies from about 57'5" and 1°01'10". The Moon's arc is much larger, between about 11 and 14 degrees per day. Each of the planets has a variable arc speed depending on forward and retrograde motion. For the purposes of discussion in this article, directions involve the actual motion of Mercury measured in longitude.

When learning to use arc directions, the student must take into account the direction of the forward and converse arcs for any given date. The arcs occasionally appear to move backward or forward together, and sometimes the forward arc moves backward through the zodiac while the converse arc moves forward. By examining the ephemeris for the days and months before and after birth, you can easily determine the apparent motion of the forward and converse directions. Using Intrepid or other software, you can observe the motion of the arc direction this way:

- Construct a triwheel with natal converse and forward arcs.
- Move the time forward or backward in Intrepid's "keypad."
- Watch the arc wheels turn independent of the birth chart and each other on the screen.

With planetary arc directions, the view is from the Earth. The different arcs, however, reflect the qualities of the planet being tracked. Solar arc directions reflect the course of individual human life. Lunar and planetary arcs focus on specific qualities of our lives that are closely associated with the particular archetypal nature of the Moon or planets. It is as if you are lifted out of your typical person-centered mentality and offered a clearer understanding of the world based on a selected planetary archetype. Mercury relates to communication, documents, travel, and health.

Why Dueling Arc Directions?

Research of numerous charts indicates that aspects between the forward and converse arc charts reflect the most poignant events in life. When looking at difficult events, very often conjunctions signal the end or beginning of great adventures, while squares and oppositions indicate major challenges or shifts in awareness. Typically these events reflect the impact at the time of the event as it relates to the past. It's a matter of Karma meeting Dharma. Forward and converse arcs, taken together, highlight the essential drama when current or future events depend in some way on past actions.

The U.S. Chart and Individual Lives: The Constructive Side of the Civil Rights Debate in the United States

Civil rights issues have been around since colonial times in the U.S. Forefathers like Thomas Jefferson owned slaves. Although Jefferson only freed two slaves during his lifetime, he had written into the *Declaration of Independence* some remarks about abolishing slave trade between Great Britain and the colonies. That language was removed, leaving the familiar statement that "all men are created equal" and endowed with rights.

Throughout U.S. history the themes of human rights and slavery have arisen again and again. Numerous efforts have been made to confirm the sentiment of the *Declaration of Independence* and the *Constitution*. Among them are these events:

- The original Bill of Rights (ten constitutional amendments to clarify our founders' intentions) ratified December 15, 1791
- End of Importation of Slaves March 2, 1807
- Abraham Lincoln Inaugurated March 4, 1861
- Slavery was abolished in 1865 (13th amendment to the constitution) December 6, 1865
- Citizenship for all people was legislated in 1868 (14th amendment) July 9, 1868
- The universal right for men (15th amendment) February 3, 1870
- Women's Suffrage (19th Amendment) August 18, 1920
- Lyndon Johnson Sworn In November 22, 1963
- Civil Rights Act of 1964 July 2, 1964
- Voting Rights Act 1965 August 6, 1965
- Lunar Launch 1969 July 16, 1969, 9:32 a.m.
- Walk on the Moon 1969 July 20, 1969 10:56 p.m.

At least sixteen of twenty-six amendments to the constitution relate directly to individual rights of citizens. This fact alone should convince the reader that civil rights issues have an enduring place in U.S. history and law. Where constitutional amendment was not necessary or possible, Congress has passed significant legislation that shows the lengths government has gone to in order to assure some degree of equality for citizens (and by extension others who reside in the U.S.).

How Planetary Arcs Work

The graphic below illustrates how Mercury arc directions work differently from solar arc directions. All planetary arc directions share similar phenomena.

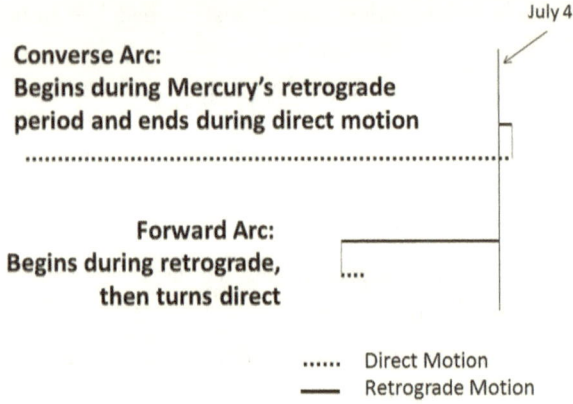

Mercury Arc Directions
(motion from July 4, 1776 to 1800)

The solid lines represent the period before and after the signing of the Declaration of Independence when Mercury was retrograde. The longer dotted line represents the expected direction of motion of the converse Mercury arc in the years following the Declaration of Independence. The shorter dotted line represents direct motion of the forward Mercury arc from 1794 to 1800, as seen in day per year motion after July 4, 1776.

Impact of Natal Mercury Retrograde in the U.S. Chart

With Mercury retrograde at the signing of the Declaration of Independence, some tough times lay ahead in terms of actually accomplishing independence. Having already been engaged in the war for over a year, the fight would continue until October 19, 1781, when General Cornwallis surrendered at the Battle of Yorktown, Virginia.

The British House of Commons voted to end the American war in April of 1782. The preliminary articles of the Treaty of Paris were signed in late November 1782, and the final treaty was signed on September 3, 1783. By October 1781, the U.S. converse Mercury arc was barely moving one minute per year, and it changed direction in May of 1783, about midway between the initial signing and the final treaty.

Meanwhile, the forward arc Mercury continued to retrograde, stationing to resume direct motion in mid-1994. This was right at the peak of resistance during the Whiskey Rebellion, a protest against excise taxation of whiskey to raise funds for the new nation. Also, in 1794 the Eleventh Amendment was passed (March 4), overthrowing a Supreme Court decision and establishing state's rights.

The motion of arc directed Mercury arcs in early U.S. history reflects the progress of the Revolutionary War, establishment of the nation, financing government, and recognizing state's rights. These complex matters required repeated re-visitation of the constitution, as we might expect from actions taken under Mercury retrograde.

Civil Rights Legislation

End of Importation of Slaves

My first example of Mercury arcs is March 2, 1807, the date of passage of legislation to ban the importation of slaves into the United States. The law actually went into effect on January 1, 1808.

Note in both charts that the forward Mercury arc, after its earlier retrograde motion, has almost returned to Mercury's natal position on the date the legislation was signed into law (the exact return was two months later). This conjunction result in both charts occurs because Mercury has only a tiny amount of motion during the fifteen minutes of clock time between the two charts,

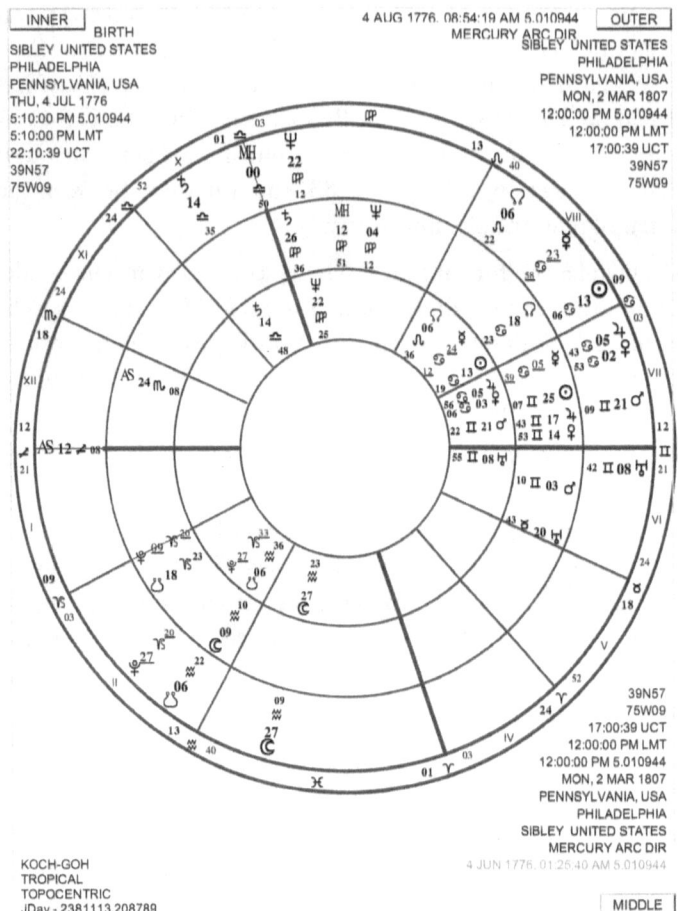

and therefore the Mercury arcs are virtually identical. Changes among aspects to the angles are the only factors to examine in terms of testing the two birth times.

Sibley Chart

In addition to the multiple conjunctions already noted, in the Sibley chart we find two aspects between the forward and converse charts involving the angles with orbs of less than 15' of arc. Here and throughout this article, I will be quoting Ebertin's

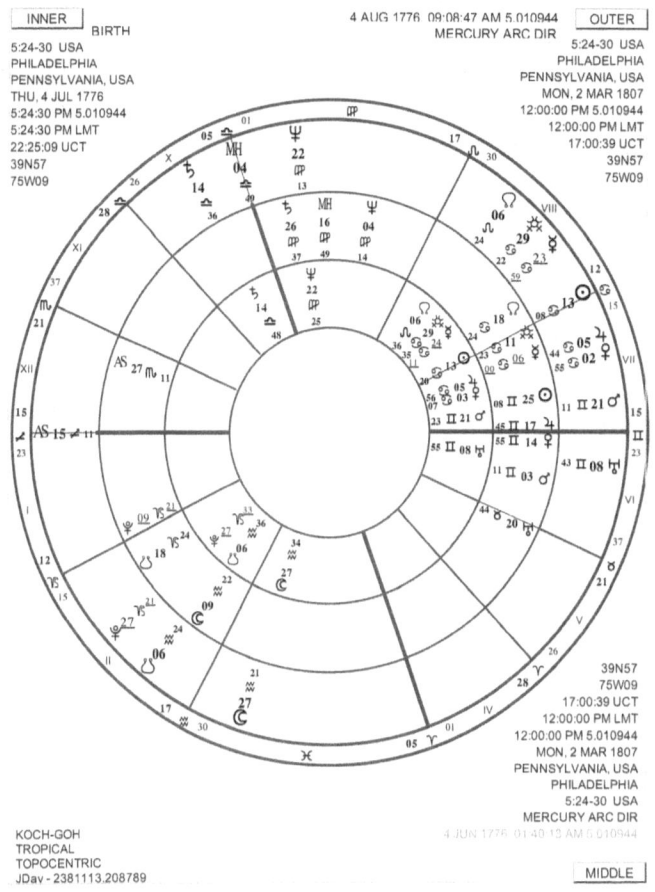

Combination of Stellar Influences for brief delineations of aspects (in bold type).

- Forward Mercury trine the converse Ascendant (10')is the closest forward to converse aspect to an angle. Ebertin mentions **receiving documents**, which is exactly what the nation did—it received a document declaring a new law.

- The forward Sun sextile converse Midheaven (15') suggest an opportunity (sextile) to confirm the nation's **conscious** objectives and **positive outlook on life**.

- Additionally, the converse Ascendant trines natal Mercury (4') indicates something from the past (converse) that brings **personal attitudes** into play amid the **receiving of documents, and the desire to chat with people**.

Close Chart

We find four aspects to the angles in the Close chart within 15' of orb:

- Forward Ascendant opposition converse Venus (15')—**embellishment**
- Forward Moon square converse Ascendant (10')—**disharmony in relationships**
- Forward Pluto sextile converse Ascendant (9')—**readjustment of conditions through rule over the environment**
- Converse Ascendant biquintile Venus (4')—**embellishment**

These aspects describe the situation quite well: the laws of the nation were embellished through addition. There was a lot of disharmony among the legislators leading up to this enactment, and plenty of disharmony afterward. However, the power of the U.S. government to enact laws that affect all of the states was confirmed. This law responded to the earlier state's rights issue to override the blanket state's rights granted in the Eleventh Amendment. Although the state's rights issue is a side track for this article, it seems good to note that the retrograde process of revising laws started early and continues to this day. Finally, The U.S. made an early effort to improve its position on the international scene.

Back to the point: The Close chart includes more aspects involving the angles, and provides ample confirmation of the nature of the event. Still, the differences between the two U.S. chart times are not yet compelling, although the Close chart has more aspects with very narrow orbs.

- No forward arc to converse arc aspects to the angles within 20 minutes orb
- Forward arc Ascendant square natal Mars (2')
- No converse arc to natal aspects within 30' orb

Aspects in the Close chart include:
- Forward arc Midheaven semisquare converse Venus (11')
- Forward arc Ascendant trine natal Mercury (10')
- Forward arc North Node semisextile natal Ascendant (12')
- No converse to natal aspects to angles

There are numerous interplanetary aspects in the two U.S. charts, including:
- Forward Venus biquintile converse Neptune (0')
- Forward Jupiter biquintile converse Sun (6')
- Forward Saturn semisquare converse Sun (14')
- Forward Uranus trine Neptune (12')
- Forward Neptune sextile Jupiter (13')

The importance of the moment is shown well in planetary aspects; aspects involving the angles are stronger in the Close chart.

Women's Suffrage: Amendment 1920

There is only one aspect within orb in the Sibley chartm, while the Close chart has four.

In researching the issue of women's suffrage, I was reminded twenty-three states allowed women to vote for the President before 1920, and that fourteen states had full suffrage before that date. Thus the issues were remarkably similar to those of the 1870 situation for men, although the 1870 amendment was ostenSibley more about race and the 1920 amendment about sex. Once again the federal government stepped in to amend the Constitution in favor of all humans, not just men or white men.

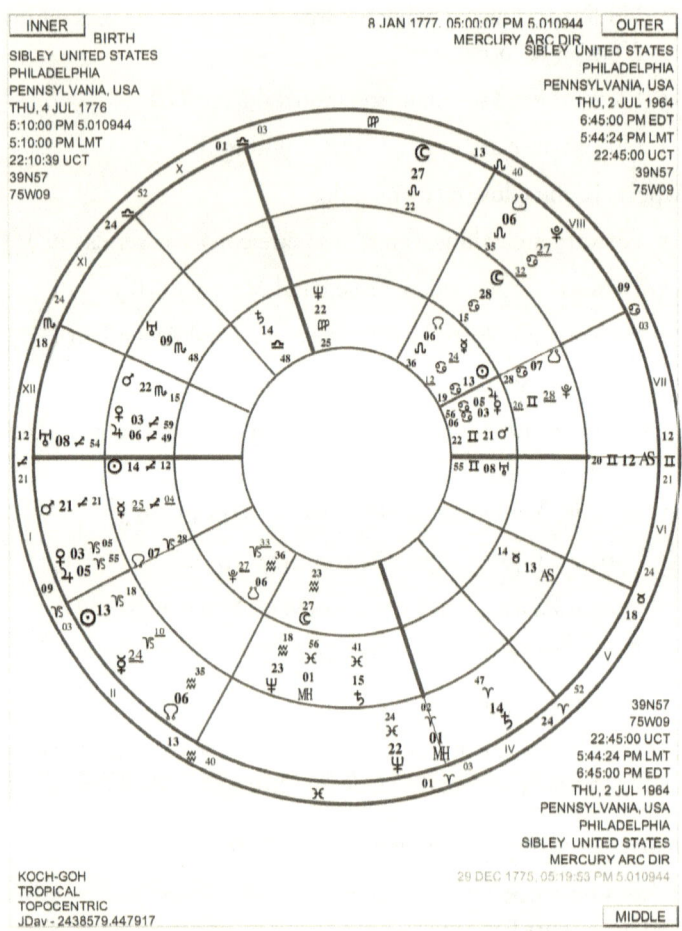

Civil Right Act of 1964

This civil rights legislation was already in motion before Johnson assumed office. In fact, he had been instrumental in the forging (some would say dilution of) a law proposed by Eisenhower in 1957 to mend voting rights differences among the states, and he avidly supported the 1964 law.

Recall that these arc charts are for Mercury arcs. I chose Mercury arcs because the Civil Rights Bill is a document (Mercury). I ex-

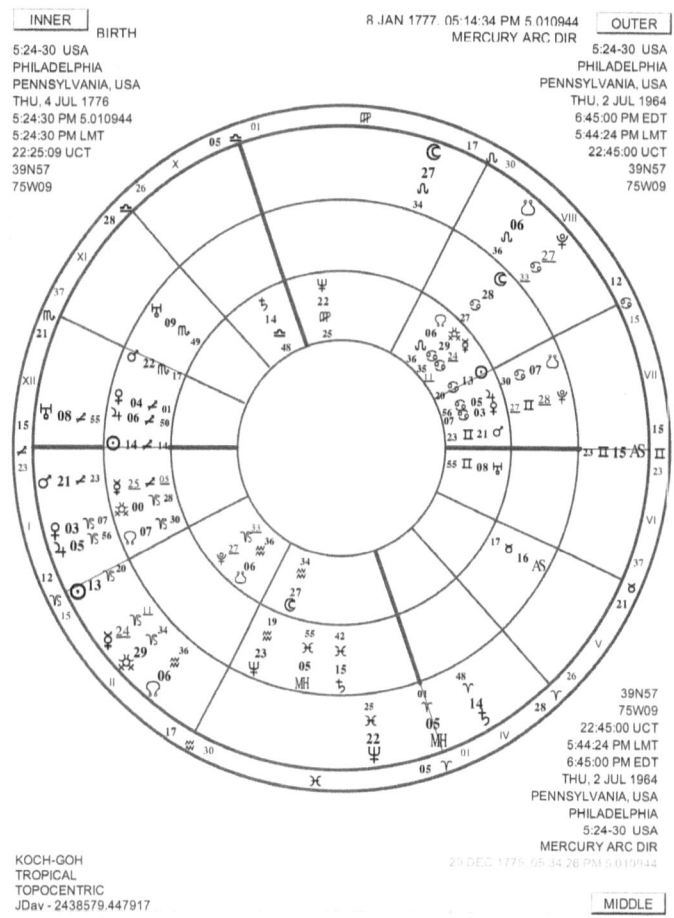

pected to find Jupiter/ninth house involvement (law in general) or Saturn (modern ruler Uranus)/eleventh house legislation.

PosSibley the most notable fact is that the forward Mercury arc has reached exact opposition. This would be true for anyone born or any organization begun on July 4, 1776. (The U.S. is the only such entity I know of that is still in existence.) The converse Mercury arc, in contrast, has reached a quincunx aspect to the natal (not as close to exact). These aspects are identical in both the Sibley and Close charts.

For purposes of delineation, we could probably stop here. Regardless of the U.S. birth time question, the Mercury arcs on this date show that the Civil Rights Act of 1964 represents one of those watershed moments when the nation is fully aware of its values.

- The Forward arc Midheaven in Aries reflects **intense awareness of objectives in life** contrasting via the opposition to the birth Midheaven in Libra suggesting **adaptation**.

- Natal Jupiter in Cancer signifies a **sense of justice**. Forward arc Jupiter in Capricorn reflects a **sense of responsibility and duty**.

- Natal Ascendant in Sagittarius suggests **a society with great and far-reaching aims**. The Forward arc Ascendant in Gemini reflects **adaptation** again, a theme of the times.

Reminiscent of the original Mercury retrograde in the U.S. chart, even this legislation needed subsequent help to boost its effectiveness!

Further Analysis of Sibley and Close Charts for the 1964 Date

Considering *aspects of the angles to planets* and vice versa between the forward and converse arc charts, in the Sibley chart we find the forward Sun trine converse Ascendant aspect (4') and converse Ascendant sextile the natal Sun, suggesting **advancement of [the nation's interests]**. The Sibley chart, then, focuses attention on the executive signature (Sun).

In the Close chart we find forward arc Jupiter within 1' of the exact sextile to the converse Midheaven, and converse Midheaven trines natal Jupiter, just as the Ascendant to Sun aspects in the Sibley chart but with incredibly tight orbs. The Jupiter / Midheaven combination suggests **consciousness of aim or objective in life, and the attainment of success.**

Here we see another case where the Close chart reveals tighter orbs involving the angles. In both the Sibley and Close charts, the closest aspects are so-called soft aspects—trines, sextiles, and so on. Decisive action, however, is well framed in the forward Midheaven square birth Jupiter, and also the forward Jupiter sextile converse Midheaven, two virtually exact aspects.

Lyndon Johnson

I went deeper into this event to consider Lyndon Johnson's birth chart. He was actively involved in pushing this legislation through congress, as he had been with previous similar legislation, and he signed the bill into law. In comparing Johnson's Mercury arcs to the U.S. charts, we find some remarkable connections.

Johnson's forward arc Ascendant and North Node form a yod with his converse arc Midheaven, suggesting this was a karmic or evolutionary moment in his life. The forward Ascendant to converse Midheaven quincunx has a 0 degree orb. All three points aspect the Midheaven in the Close natal and Mercury arc charts for the 1964 event. Johnson's converse Midheaven is well within one degree of conjunction to the forward arc Midheaven and opposite the natal Midheaven in the Close chart. Johnson's forward Moon squares his converse Saturn, another indicator of the karmic challenge. Both planets aspect the 13 degree Sun in the U.S. chart. Johnson's converse Mars and forward Sun are in the same degree (different signs) as all three Midheavens in the Close chart, reflecting the action of signing the bill.

Sibley U.S. Chart and Johnson

Do we find the same level of connection between Johnson and the Sibley chart? Johnson's forward arc Midheaven is well past aspects to the Midheavens in the Sibley chart. That is not surprising, considering the fact that Johnson had been working for this legislation for quite some time. Johnson's forward Moon, forward Mercury and converse Saturn form tight aspects to the

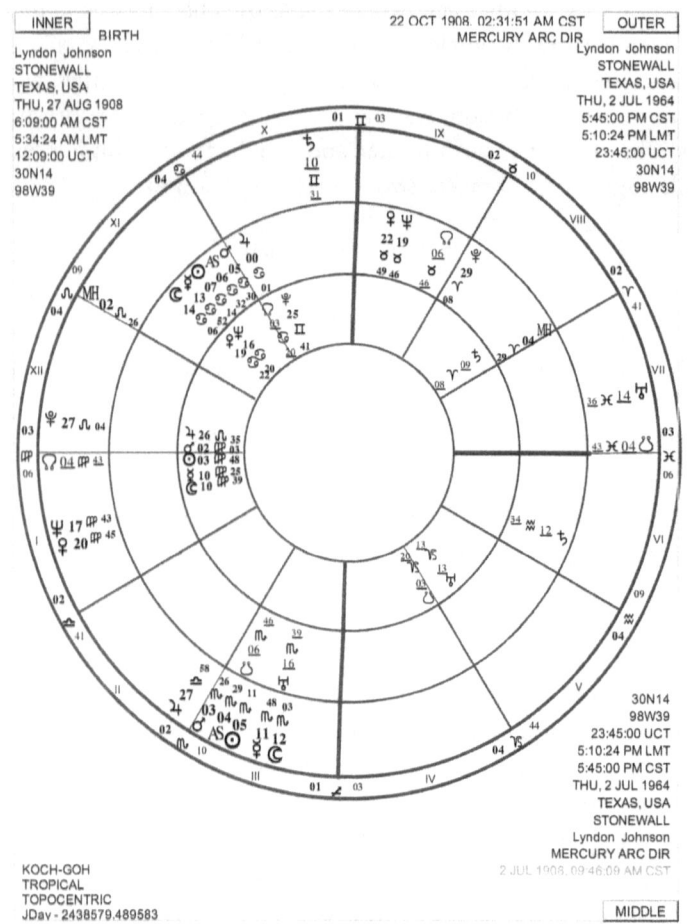

Sibley U.S. Ascendant.

Reminder: the planetary aspects between the two U.S. charts do not change significantly. This phenomenon often occurs when rectifying natal charts, where the only big changes over short periods of time are the angles.

In both charts Johnson's forward Uranus is square the converse U.S. Sun and quincunx the natal U.S. Saturn; and his converse Moon also occupies the 14th degree, opposing his natal Uranus and conjunct the U.S. Sun. These and other planetary aspects certainly reflect the connection between Johnson and the U.S. during his presidency and particularly at the time of this legislation, regardless of which U.S. birth time we use.

Voting Rights Act of 1965

Pursuant to the implementation of the Civil Rights Act of 1964, a law was enacted on August 5, 1965 to ensure that voting rights were observed in all of the states equally. Because the Civil Rights Act of 1964 had an enforcement clause, the Voting Rights Act had real "teeth" to act in specific states and jurisdictions. This law has been renewed four times (it originally had an expiry date).

For this law the Sibley and Close charts have the same number of aspects to the angles within the 15' orb.

Neil Armstrong's Walk on the Moon

As a test of this admittedly limited analysis of two potential U.S. charts, Neil Armstrong's walk on the Moon is a sterling example. The results for the Mercury arced chart are in the tablulation. Here, though, I have chosen to look at the solar arc chart for the U.S. and the Lunar arc chart for Armstrong, as he was on the Moon.

These anecdotal charts have a curiously compelling feature. We find:

- Forward solar arc Mars conjunct converse arc Sun (**consciousness of the objective; successes**)
- Forward arc South Node conjunct converse arc Moon (**emotional attitude toward associations [with groups]**)
- In the Close chart we also find Forward arc Sun sextile converse arc Midheaven (**will, vitality, extraordinary achievements**)

A poignant fact is that in Armstrong's Lunar arc chart for the event, we find the exact same three aspect combinations: Mars

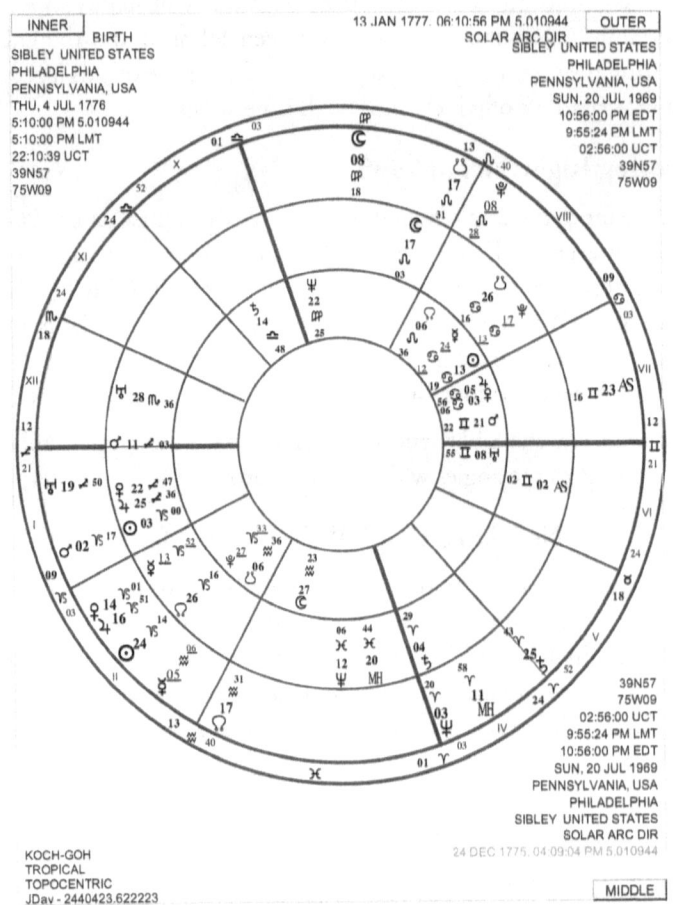

to South Node, Sun to Moon, and Midheaven to Sun. The nation and Armstrong had the same karma to dharma experiences on that day! For planet Earth, the walk on the Moon signaled the potential to explore space. For Neil Armstrong, the event marked a date when he experienced the smallness of himself in comparison to the Earth and to the universe. This was a life-changing event for him, and billions of people shared vicariously in that moment.

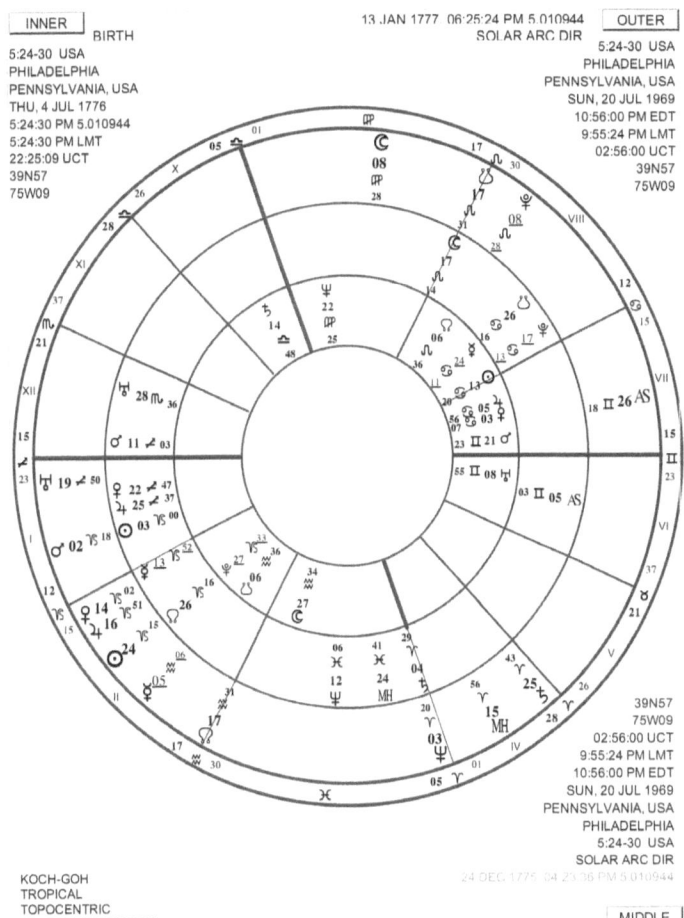

One outgrowth of the Apollo missions was the "Blue Marble" pictures of the earth. The astronauts fell in love with the earth in a whole new way when they saw her from space, and this symbol of who we are has endured, perhaps as much as any other. It underlies ongoing efforts to heal and preserve the planet, and it definitely has encouraged my study of planet-centered perspectives in astrology. With Mars landers exploring and sending images back to us as I write this article, we can anticipate a time when people can indeed experience a different planet-centered

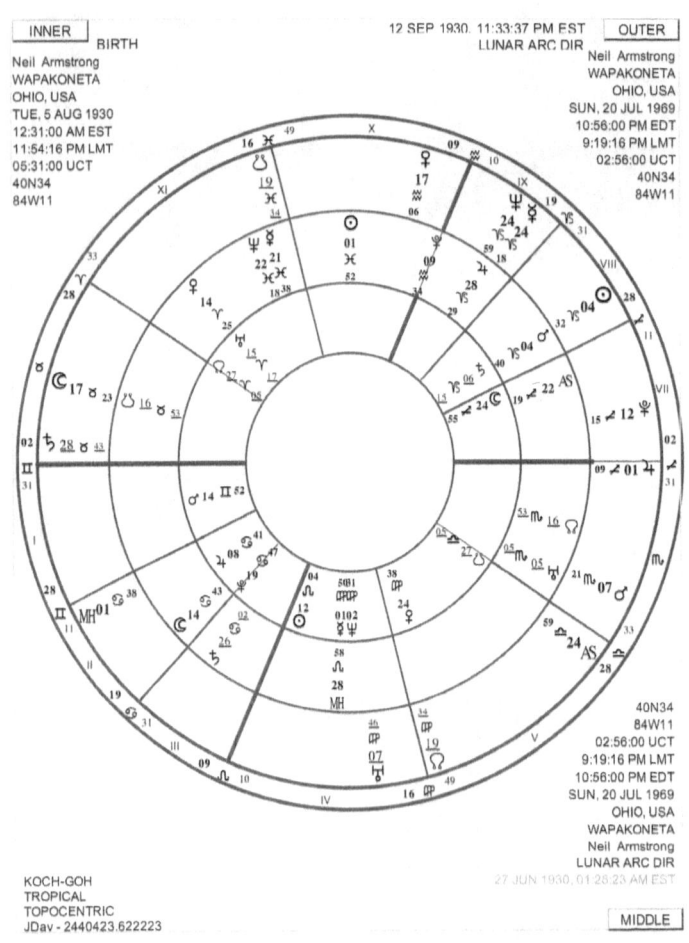

perspective.

In keeping with the Sun to Mars aspects in the above charts, I have included Neil Armstrong's Mars-centered chart (exemplifying the archetypal energy of courage and independence of the Apollo program and Armstrong's life as an astronaut), along with transits for the moment he stepped onto the lunar surface.

Within ten minutes before the historic "first step," transiting Deimos conjuncted the Mars-centered Jupiter (**successful enter-**

Planetary Arc Directions

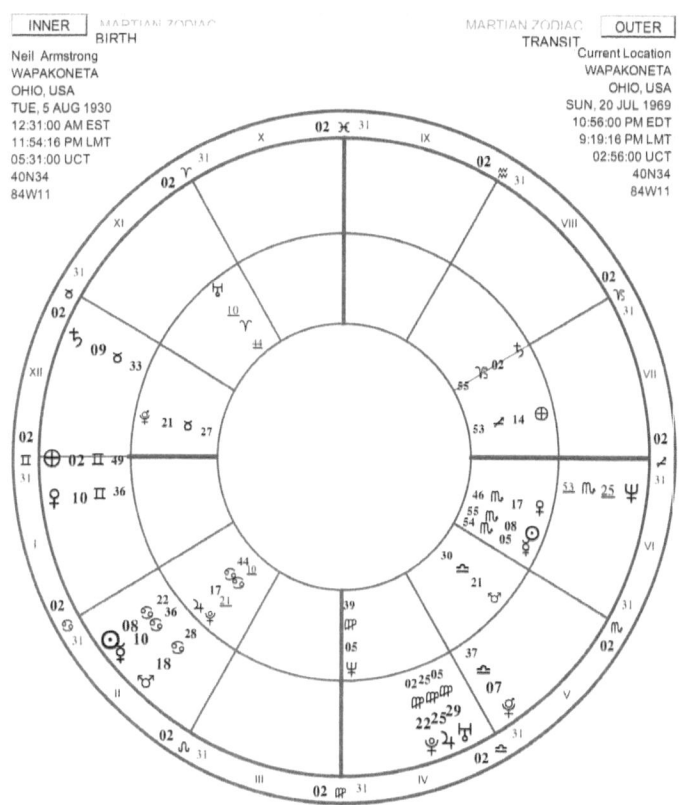

EQUAL
MARTIAN
GEOCENTRIC
JDav - 2440423.622223

prise). Within five minutes after, Phobos formed a semisextile to the Sun (**advancement; overcoming dangers**) and opposition to Uranus (**passing a test of nerves**). The moment invoked the transpersonal qualities of active compassion and intuition, not just for Neil, but for us all.

Conclusions

While this article is not extensive enough to prove the 5:24:30 time for the U.S. chart, it demonstrates the following:

- The later time for the U.S. chart yields closer aspects than the Sibley chart for the majority of these particular events.
- The use of orbs greater than one degree for progressions, directions, and transits is not only unnecessary, it is unwarranted. Triwheel charts that I have examined include ten to twelve aspects of less than one degree orb, with a rare exception (a chart for a planet not directly related to the event). When the birth time is accurate, aspects for significant event dates are within minutes of exactitude.
- Forward and converse arc directions, when taken together to a birth chart, provide compelling event delineations, based on the nature of the planetary arc used.
- Finally, unlike Ebertin's work with solar arcs, these charts demonstrate the value of including so-called soft aspects, particularly when researching so-called creative or "fun" events.

Recommendations for Additional Research

Comparable data for the enactment of other laws and amendments, including those later repealed, would form a body of data suitable for expanded research into the efficacy of Forward and Converse Mercury arc directions. Comparable data from other countries would be useful as well.

Similarly, a carefully documented list of events in an individual's life, selected for their common planetary archetypal themes, would form additional bodies of research of other planetary arcs.

Any body of data that relates to one planetary archetype could be used for research into planetary arc directions (or planet-centered astrology).

Tabulation of Aspects within 15' Orb

Using the Sibley and Close U.S. charts, the number of aspects within 15' orb is listed. The aspects were calculated between:

- Forward and converse arcs
- Forward arc and natal
- Converse arc and natal

In the case of amendments to the Constitution, the date of ratification is used. In the case of legislation, the date of signing into law is used. Aspects were considered *only* for the Midheaven and Ascendant. There are numerous interplanetary aspects, but they have no bearing on the birth time differences.

Bill of Rights Ratified, December 15, 1791
Sibley Chart Aspects: 2
Close Chart Aspects: 4
Difference: +
Notes: Forward to natal conjunction within 1°1' orb

End Importation of Slaves, March 2, 1807
Sibley Chart Aspects: 3
Close Chart Aspects: 4
Difference: +

Lincoln Inauguration, March 4, 1861
Sibley Chart Aspects: 4
Close Chart Aspects: 2
Difference: -

Slavery Abolished, December 6, 1865
Sibley Chart Aspects: 1
Close Chart Aspects: 3
Difference: +

Citizenship Regardless of Race, July 9, 1868
Sibley Chart Aspects: 1
Close Chart Aspects: 6
Difference: +

Suffrage for Men, February 3, 1870
Sibley Chart Aspects: 4
Close Chart Aspects: 7
Difference: +

Suffrage for Women, August 18, 1920
  Sibley Chart Aspects: 1
  Close Chart Aspects: 4
  Difference: +
  Notes: Converse to natal wheel sesquisquare

Johnson Sworn in as President, November 22, 1963
  Sibley Chart Aspects: 3
  Close Chart Aspects: 5
  Difference: +
  Notes: Forward to natal opposition (wide orb)

Civil Rights Act, July 2, 1964
  Sibley Chart Aspects: 3
  Close Chart Aspects: 2
  Notes: Forward to natal opposition (1'orb!)

Voting Rights Act, August 6, 1965
  Sibley Chart Aspects: 6
  Close Chart Aspects: 6
  Difference: same

Launch Lunar Lander, July 16, 1960
  Sibley Chart Aspects: 8
  Close Chart Aspects: 1
  Difference: -
  Notes: Forward to converse wheel semisquare

Lunar Landing, July 20, 1969
  Sibley Chart Aspects: 7
  Close Chart Aspects: 3
  Difference: -
  Notes: Forward to converse wheel semisquare

An Astrological Perspective on Women's Rights Issues

By Marilyn J Muir LPMAFA

The rights of women and families are a high priority in U.S. politics at this time, including an onslaught of roll-back-the-clock legislation, with state legislatures enacting restrictions on family planning, birth control, women's health, invasive pelvic procedures, abortion, the rights of an embryonic life form, rape, and more. These state-level actions are paralleled by multiple congressional abortion bills, personhood attempts, and limiting women's health care access. Why is there such a drive to repeal the hard-won rights of women and families? Why is there such a battle between revisiting the past and moving into the future? Why is there such a polarization between the sides of the issues? Why such extreme, such invasive, and such punitive measures?

Polarization

It is not difficult to remember the recent Saturn-Uranus opposition in Virgo-Pisces that seems to have set this current polarization in motion. Just because the aspect itself is completed does not mean the lessons are complete. Think of brewng a pot of coffee: the process is not finished when the water is boiled; that is the energizing part, the actual aspect. The boiling water has to pass through the grounds before it becomes coffee. Similarly, the energy released by the aspect has to percolate through human experience before we are able to define its effects.

The Saturn-Uranus opposition was a long aspect even if you consider only the perfect aspects, but we all know about orb. The surrounding effects lasted over a long period and the aspect itself even moved into Libra-Aries to add flavor and complicate interpretation. This aspect is still brewing, years later.

Saturn represents tradition, conservative behavior, responsibility, form, and structure. Uranus represents the cutting edge, the forward motion of life called evolution, breakthrough energy, and what is new. We are creatures of habit; we resist change. But evolution itself is a progressive, forward motion. To move backward is to devolve–nothing we should wish to do. If we as a species devolve we will become a footnote in history instead of a driving force of nature itself. Think on this.

Extremism

What about the Uranus-Pluto square that seems to be wreaking havoc in our world? Wars, rumors of wars, extremism of all kinds. Every kind of human foible seems to be center stage and this is not going to go away quickly just because it is uncomfortable to us. This aspect still has time to trigger all sorts of difficult experiences because it is still in the active stage. As this aspect begins to separate we will have to sort through these experiences.

Such major energies are universal in nature and our small planet spins continually under and through these energies, constantly absorbing and experiencing what these energies provoke. This is a given, a common factor to all life on this planet.

Chart for Women's Issues

What are the astrological indications that point to a women's/family conflict? To begin, we need a natal chart, so I searched through history.

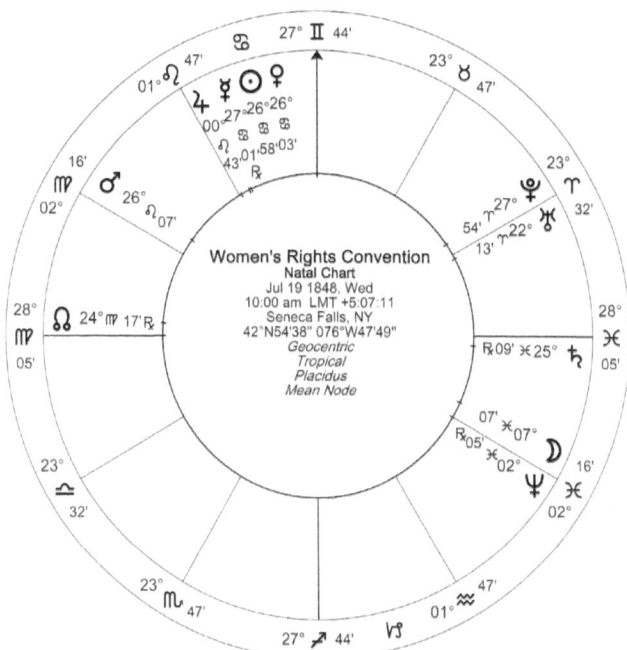

The first relatively modern activation for the women's movement (there were other previous attempts) appears to be the first conference on women's rights that was held in Seneca Falls, New York on July 19, 1848; the Wikipedia article gives a reference to 10:00 am LMT. I was shocked to see the date 1848, because I knew I had a trustworthy chart.

I had recently researched the history of Wisconsin and California statehoods and current events because these two states are experiencing their first Neptune return. Wisconsin's birth year is 1848. Mexico ceded California to the U.S. by treaty in 1848. The modern women's rights movement began in 1848. Neptune returns for all three are active.

The women's movement is experiencing a Neptune return, and because this is an aspect than can occur only once in 164.7 years, give or take a little for retrogrades and orb, this is an incredibly important trigger. Since states and countries have a lifetime beyond the human life span, these charts provide examples that can help us to understand the concept of a Neptune return: discovery (not invention) turns an unconscious (invisible) energy into a conscious (visible) energy so that we can visibly observe what has always been an unconscious energy.

The 1848 convention chart has Neptune at 2 Pisces 05 retrograde. Transiting Neptune moved into Pisces on April 4, 2011, just after the 2010 election and the 2011 swearing-in of the new Congress, state legislators, and governors. The War on Women began and legislative action rolling back women's/family issues and rights struck in full force. Transiting Neptune's early foray into Pisces lasted until August 5, 2011, when it retrograded into late Aquarius, still well within orb of the women's rights chart natal Neptune. On February 3, 2012, Neptune moved fully into Pisces with its journey through Aquarius complete. Pisces is the sign of Neptune's rulership, in dignity and strong, It danced all the way up to 3 Pisces 09, turning retrograde on June 4, 2012. It then stationed direct at 0 Pisces 22 on November 11, 2012, five days after the election. Great timing.

When a planet stations, it pulses in a tiny sliver of space, more powerful than when it is moving at its "normal" pace. Think of how much energy is pulsing into that tiny sliver of space, how powerfully that point in space is irradiated, and how strong the influence could be in a chart. As previously stated, unknown or less understood does not equate to unimportant.

A powerful and unusual (164.7 years) planetary return with incredibly powerful and important stations is triggering the women's rights chart now. Neptune continued its journey to 5 Pisces 23 on June 7, 2013, and then retrograded to 2 Pisces 35 on November 13, 2013, well within orb of aspect. Our key point for women's issues is 2 Pisces 05 retrograde, and the triggering of this point actually finished on February 1, 2013, about ten days after the presidential inauguration. This highlighted the poten-

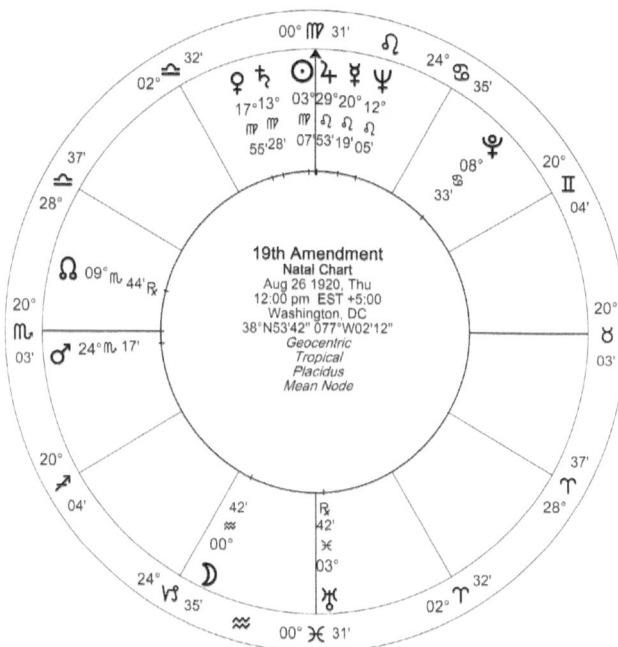

tial for influence and effect on the variety of current women's/family issues yet to come to completion.

As part of my research I have started a year-by-year progressed spreadsheet of the events that have occurred since 1848, including the 19th Amendment to the U.S. Bill of Rights. The Sun for this amendment is at 3 Virgo 07, with Uranus at 3 Pisces 42 retrograde. This means that transiting Neptune activated the Amendment Sun-Uranus in 2013, so women had better pay attention to their constitutional rights.

It will be another 164.7 years before women's rights issues will be activated by the next Neptune return. You and I will not be around to witness it, but we can hope to leave an understanding of it to our descendents.

For further research you can find a timeline and more information at www.infoplease.com/spot/womenstimeline1.html.

More Transits

Transiting Saturn was also activating the women's rights chart. With natal Sun 26 Cancer 58, retrograde Mercury at 27 Cancer 01, Venus at 26 Cancer 03, Uranus at 22 Aries 13, and Pluto at 27 Aries 54, transiting Saturn in late Libra was square the Cancer positions and opposition the Aries positions, creating a T-square battle of five of the ten natal planetary positions. These positions tie in closely to the U.S. natal retrograde Mercury at 24 Cancer 20 and natal retrograde Pluto at 27 Capricorn 33. This sums up today's issues: traditional, conservative, and at times dictatorial Saturn playing out in a very visible political war on women through Saturn triggering the T-square and collective grand cross. Who represents Saturn? The political right. Who or what is under assault? The natal and progressed planets of the Women's Rights movement.

To complete that transiting picture, Uranus was in early Aries and Pluto was in early Capricorn, neither triggering anything in particular in the women's rights chart. So action was generated by both Neptune and Saturn, who are not necessarily the best of friends.

Neptune represents the spiritual essence of a person, a country, or a movement. The return of Neptune to its original position triggered the initial spiritual essence with an awakening of a current spiritual essence. My curiosity ran away with me, as often happens, and I did the year-by-year progressions for the entire 165 years. Progressed retrograde Neptune turned direct circa 1963 in late Aquarius and for 2012 was at 0 Pisces 30. Transiting Neptune moved back and forth across 0 Pisces 30 to 2 Pis 06, finishing its passage on February 2, 2013. It did retrograde within a half degree of the natal position in mid-November 2013, but did not complete the activation.

Are women truly awake and aware (Neptune return) of the threat to their rights visible in the women's rights natal chart? I hope so, because the completion of this Neptune return and the

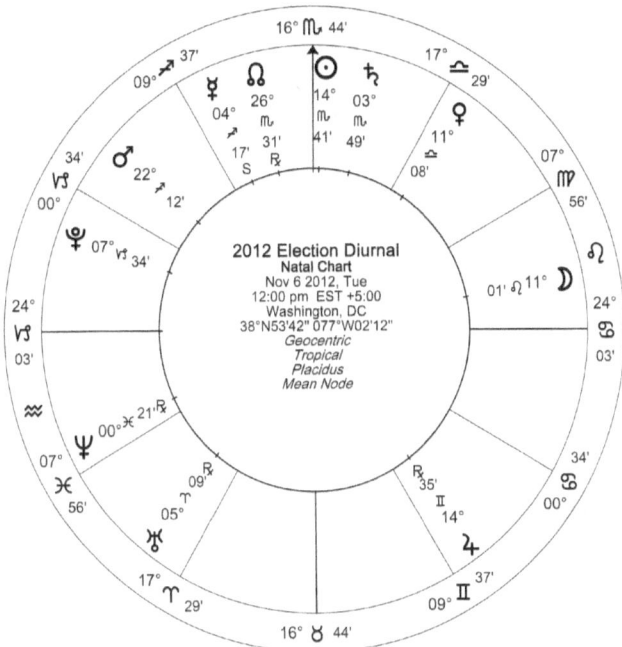

final activation of Saturn to the cardinal positions happened. The Saturn/right-wing onslaught has done whatever damage it can do to women's rights. Was any female listening? Are we willing to join those courageous women of 1848 to defend our own rights or will we let ourselves be conned or lulled into the passive acceptance that would be negative Neptune?

More to Come

Do not let your guard down yet if you think the activation is finished. The women's rights chart natal Moon is at 7 Pisces 07, and thus a quintuple activation awaits us in 2014 and 2015. This is not yet a done deal.

The 19th Amendment chart has the Sun at 3 Virgo 07 opposition retrograde Uranus at 3 Pisces 42, so transiting Neptune triggered the Sun-Uranus opposition. Could our lax attitude on this attack on our assumed rights jeopardize the 19th Amendment and all it represents to women? Needless to say I spent some time on the transits and the progressions of this whole complex: our country, the Women's Rights Convention, the 19th Amendment, and the 2012 election. Following are some of the results:

- U.S. chart (July 4, 1776, 9:36 am, Philadelphia) progressed to the 19th Amendment has the Sun at 4 Sagittarius 08, the Moon at 7 Gemini 31 (Full Moon), and retrograde Uranus at 9 Gemini 09, all of which are activated during 2013-15.
- The 19th Amendment progressed Sun was at 4 Sagittarius 22.
- Progressed Uranus was at 1 Pisces 51, dancing with transiting Neptune.
- The 2012 election chart (November 6, 2012) and diurnals have Mercury at 4 Sagittarius 17 and retrograde Neptune at 4 Pisces 21, a tight square activating the four-degree mutable positions.

The following are aspects to the 19th Amendment chart:

- Transiting Neptune opposition natal Sun on February 28, 1013, September 29, 2013, and December 27, 2013.
- Transiting Neptune conjunct natal Uranus on March 17, 2013, September 5, 2013, and January 17, 2014.
- Transiting Neptune square the progressed Sun on May 6, 2013, August 12, 2013, and February 6, 2014.
- Transiting Neptune conjunct progressed Uranus on February 2, 2012, August 20, 2012, and January 25, 2013.
- Transiting Pluto opposition natal Pluto February 7, 2012, June 18, 2012, and December 10, 2012.
- Transiting Pluto opposition progressed Pluto on December 8, 2012.
- Transiting Pluto opposition progressed Venus five times in

2013-14: March 3, May 24, and December 29, 2013, and August 27 and October 10, 2014.

- Transiting Uranus square Pluto on July 13, 2012 (station), March 30, 2013, and December 17, 2013.
- Transiting Uranus square progressed Pluto, ending March 29, 2013.
- Transiting Uranus square progressed Venus on May 19 and September 17, 2013, and March 10, 2014.
- Transiting Sat square natal Mercury on December 31, 2013, May 8, 2014, and September 29, 2014.
- Transiting Saturn square Jupiter on December 22, 2014, June 16, 2014, and September 16, 2015.
- Transiting Saturn single passes over several fixed positions: square Neptune on October 19, 2013; square progressed Neptune on November 2, 2013, square progressed Mercury on November 23, 2013; and square Mars on November 4, 2014.

The above is a tremendous number of activations and dates from 2012 through 2015, with only the hard aspects included. The 19th Amendment is under onslaught. The rights of women that have been strongly fought for and earned are at stake. Will the women of today have the courage of the women of yesteryear?

***

Marilyn Muir is the author of Presidents of Hope and Change, *which is available from AFA. Contact her at mmuir@cfl.rr.com if you would like to receive a copy of her aspect and event spreadsheets via email.*

The Child and the Marriage Chart

By DaCosta E. Williams, FAFA

In presenting this article I am motivated by two factors: one is idle curiosity and the other is a desire to establish a better approach, understanding, and explanation of the operative linking that occurs in the marriage chart and the children born to that marriage.

For this article I will limit my topic to two points: the first child born to the marriage, and the three basic factors that may be derived from the marriage chart–that, is the Sun sign, Moon sign, and Ascendant of the first born child.

The rules, applied to twenty cases under study, are not sufficient to cover each and every case that might arise, but they are sufficient to point the way and approach to the subject.

These cases are quite well consolidated in a given year (1946), although a few cases are not in that year. This seems to place a certain emphasis on the transit of Jupiter through Libra and Scorpio, while Saturn was in the fire sign Leo, restricting love yet placing a responsibility at the same time.

Although these cases come from a small community in a given period of time, they tend to point to a national condition that was not as carefully recorded.

While the marriage data was published after the marriage, there can be a slight time variation because marriage can no better take place on time than can other events in life. However, I have used the time stated and erected the chart accordingly. The variation, if any, is only a few minutes.

Of the group of children under study, only one has died to date (June 10, 1947). He was underweight and lived only two days.

The terms used in this article are defined below:

Marriage Chart–the date, time, and place that the marriage occurred.

Natal Chart–the date, time, and place that the first child was born.

Sign House–a planet in Cancer by sign house would be the fourth, regardless of where Cancer falls on the cusp.

House Sign–a planet falling in the tenth house would always represent he house sign of the sign it was located in at the time; for example, if Taurus, it would be the house sign of the second.

Natural House Sign–for example, any planet in the seventh house is naturally Libra, in the eighth, naturally Scorpio, etc.

Opposite Natural House Sign–for example, any planet in the seventh house is naturally always opposite to the first house or Aries.

Opposite Sign House–a planet in Leo, regardless of the house location of Leo, will always be the opposite sign house of Aquarius in natural relationship and indicate the eleventh house.

Determining Factors Related to the First-Born Child

The rules I have established for determining the locations of the Sun, Moon, and Ascendant of the first child born to the marriage are founded on these principles:

1. The male partner to a marriage is represented by the Ascendant of the marriage chart, its lord, the Sun, and the planet last aspected by the Moon.

2. The female partner to a marriage is represented by the Descendant of the marriage chart, its lord, Venus, and the planet the Moon next applies to.

3. The planet Mercury in the marriage chart rules children in general and is favored when dignified, in conjunction or aspect with Venus or Jupiter, or in a fruitful sign or house.

4. The fifth house of the marriage chart has a marked connection with the first born child, as does its ruler, planets therein, or aspects to the cusp degree, especially if very close in aspect.

5. The tenth house of the marriage chart will show what will happen to the marriage and this is shown by the lord of the tenth and planets therein, as are planets aspecting the cusp of the tenth or its lord.

I state the above bases for my rule formulation so you can better judge its worth and at the same time formulate other rules, should your study require them.

The interchanging of planets and signs, as well as houses involving the Sun, Moon, and Ascendant, have a surprising connection if one has had the inclination to study family charts. The same interchanging of factors exists in the marriage chart.

A rule may seem complicated on first reading, but will simplify upon careful reading and interpretation.

A factor can be expressed in several ways to become established; by this I mean the expression of Aquarius, for example, can come through Aquarius direct by sign regardless of house location in the chart or through the sign Leo, which is opposite. Aquarius can be expressed by house location and yet the planet may not be in Aquarius or Leo, while by house it does bear an Aquarius-Leo relationship.

All aspects are the one closest if several make aspect at the same time. The aspects must be applying and I have avoided using a wider orb than five degrees.

If a planet is retrograde, its aspects must be considered in retrograde motion only.

Rules Governing the Child's Ascendant

1. The sign of house or opposite sign or house of the ruler of the marriage chart fifth house may become the child's Ascendant or Descendant.

2. The ruler of the marriage chart Midheaven can by sign or house or opposite sign or house be the Ascendant of the child.

3. The ruler of the marriage chart Descendant can by sign or house or opposite sign or house be the Ascendant of the child.

4. A planet in the fifth house of the marriage chart aspecting the Ascendant will place the child's Ascendant in Leo or Aquarius.

Rules Governing the Child's Sun

1. The ruler of the marriage chart Ascendant can by sign or house or opposite sign or house be the house or the house or sign of the child's Sun.

2. The ruler of the marriage chart Descendant can by sign or house or opposite sign or house be the sign or house of the child's Sun.

3. The sign a planet in the marriage chart holds that is directly conjunct or opposition the marriage chart Ascendant will be the Sun sign or house of the child's Sun.

4. A planet aspecting the fifth house cusp of the marriage chart by house location or sign can be the house or sign or opposite house or sign of the child's Sun.

5. The sign or opposite sign on the cusp of the fifth house of the marriage chart can hold the child's Sun or be the house or

opposite house of the Sun.

6. The ruler of the fifth house of the marriage chart by its sign or house location can be the sign or opposite sign of the child's Sun.

7. If the ruler of the fifth house of the marriage chart aspects the marriage chart Midheaven, the Midheaven or IC sign can be the child's Sun sign.

8. If the ruler of the fifth house of the marriage chart is retrograde and aspecting the marriage chart Ascendant, the sign on the marriage chart Ascendant can be the child's Sun or house of the Sun.

9. When the ruler of the fifth house of the marriage chart aspects a planet, the planet aspected by its house or sign location or opposite sign or house can be the Sun sign or house of the child.

10. When a planet in the fifth house of the marriage chart is aspecting another planet, the sign that planet is in can be the Sun sign or house or opposite sign or house of the child's Sun.

Rules Governing the Child's Moon

1. The ruler of the sign held by the marriage chart Moon can be in a sign or house or opposite sign or house held by the child's Moon. If the Moon falls in Cancer, take the planet the Moon next aspects and use its ruler.

2. The marriage chart Mercury can be in a house or opposite house or sign or opposite sign to the child's Moon.

3. The planet that Mercury in the marriage chart first aspects can indicate by house or sign or opposite house or sign the child's Moon.

4. The ruler of the house cusp of the marriage chart Mercury can be in a house or sign or opposite house or sign to the child's Moon.

5. The ruler of the fifth house of the marriage chart can be in a sign or house or opposite sign or house to the child's Moon.

6. When the ruler of the fifth house of the marriage chart aspects a planet, that planet can be in the sign or house or opposite sign or house of the child's Moon.

7. The sign or house of a planet applying to the cusp of the fifth house of the marriage chart can hold the child's Moon.

8. A planet aspecting the fifth house cusp of the marriage chart and also aspecting the marriage chart Ascendant can place the child's Moon in the first or seventh house.

9. The ruler of the marriage chart Descendant can by sign or house or opposite sign or house be the child's Moon.

10. A planet aspecting the ruler of the marriage chart Descendant can by sign or house or opposite sign or house be the sign or house of the child's Moon.

11. A planet applying in aspect to the marriage chart Ascendant can place the child's Moon in the sign of the marriage chart Ascendant, or the ruler of the marriage chart Ascendant can be in the sign or house or opposite sign or house of the child's Moon; or it could be the aspected planet.

***

Editor's Note: Although the charts used by DaCosta Williams in this study are unavailable, his findings and conclusions merit publication and can be used and tested in future research projects. DaCosta Williams, FAFA was especially interested in astrological research.

The Autopsy of an Election

By Marilyn Muir, LPMAFA

The 2012 election process was an astrological bear. I am an old hand at calling the winner over several elections, with Bush vs. Gore being the most difficult to determine before 2012. I waited until after the primaries to calculate the charts because there were just too many candidates. Casting and reading these charts is time consuming and I did not want to waste that much time on wannabes. Once the party tickets were formed for president and vice president it was time to get serious.

All four charts were alive with activity mirroring the frantic pace of the election itself. My usual way to determine a winner starts with an accurately timed birth chart with secondary progressions to the election, plus a personal diurnal of the candidate. Why the diurnal? It provides the personal transits, including an accurate Midheaven, Ascendant, and Moon. I place all three charts on one tri-wheel with the diurnal in the center, which sets the house cusps for all the charts, the natal chart in the middle wheel, and the progressions outside.

I do *not* cast the chart for the election itself because the U.S. is a huge country with a wide time zone spread, different poll opening and closing times, and mail ballots. In this article I describe hard aspects only because of limited space.

Mitt Romney

Mitt Romney's diurnal chart for election day has the following factors:

- 14 Sagittarius 56 rising with Mars in the first house at 22 Sagittarius indicates competition, aggression, and assertive action. Sagittarius is either truth-seeking or the con-artist, or as I call it, truth and consequence.
- Uranus is conjunct the fourth house cusp (IC), indicating a possible change of residence at election . . . or a whistle-stop campaign lifestyle.
- Retrograde Jupiter, the chart ruler, is at 14 Gemini 36 in the sixth house, moving away (old activity or promise not kept) from the Descendant, with both natal and progressed Uranus (upset) in the diurnal seventh hosue. Read this as the ruler of Romney's moment is weakened in the sixth house, moving away from the power of the angle.
- Because diurnal Uranus is conjunct the diurnal IC, it is opposition the diurnal Midheaven (the goal or mission). Natal and progressed Neptune (his dreams or delusions and his religion or spirituality) are conjunct the diurnal Midhaven on the tenth house side with the Midheaven applying to both. This is not a bad aspect in and of itself, but it could play out through another venue or outlet. He could receive great applause or stature within his business community or religious organization.

There is a lot of angular action, which is typical of an important day in the life of a native. In Mitt Romney's chart, however, the activity is unsettling.

- The progressed Ascendant and Saturn are conjunct natal Saturn and all are square the diurnal Saturn.
- Diurnal Uranus opposition diurnal Venus-Midheaven and natal and progressed Neptune is contentious and divisive.

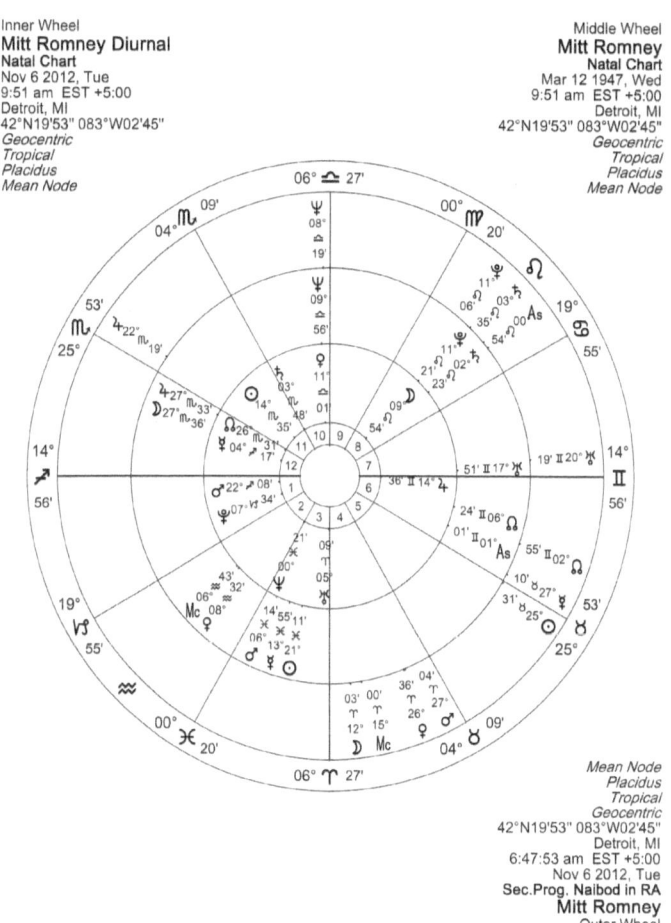

- In addition to the progressed Ascendant-Saturn, the progressed Moon is conjunct the progressed Midheaven, progressed Venus is conjunct progressed Mars, and the progressed Sun is conjunct progressed Mercury, all of which denote a good period in general but not enough to overcome the hard aspects previously mentioned. This day and the effects it produces can still benefit him as time progresses.

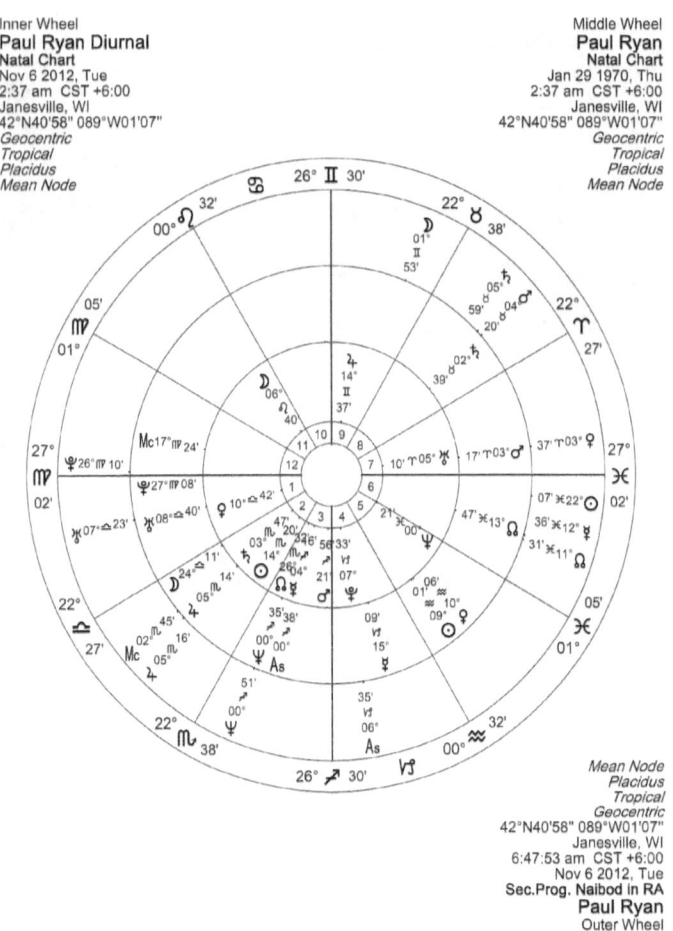

Paul Ryan

The charts have the following factors:

- The diurnal Ascendant and natal and progressed Pluto are conjunct within one degree.

- Diurnal Mars is in the third house about five degrees from the IC, which is wide to be in play.

The Autopsy of an Election

- There is an unusual Descendant conjunction between diurnal Uranus, natal Mars, and progressed Venus, which is volatile and rash; it is opposition diurnal Venus and natal and progressed Uranus in the diurnal first house. All are square diurnal Pluto and the progressed Ascendant in the diurnal fourth house.

This is not a celebratory chart, just an intensively active one.

Barack Obama

The diurnal chart has the following factors:

- Gemini rising with Jupiter about four degrees into the first house is very promising. However, Jupiter rules the seventh house of his rival and the chart ruler is retrograde Mercury in Sagittarius in the sixth house: again, not the best of placements. Do we look at Jupiter rising as yes, or is that the ruler of his rival's yes?

- Retrograde Mercury can also indicate that he goes back to do what he has done before, a second term. Could this retrograde Mercury indicate a repeat of what has happened previously?

- Diurnal Neptune is conjunct the diurnal Midheaven with natal Uranus-Node and progressed Uranus-Node in opposition and square natal Midheaven-IC; this is not the happiest of combinations.

What about his physical location?

- Natal and progressed Node-Uranus straddle the diurnal IC (again, possible whistle-stop activity), with diurnal Neptune on the tenth house side of the Midheaven.

- The progressed Ascendant at 22 Aries will form an opposition with progressed Mars-Mercury in about four years, which should equate to his vacating the office and relocating (a third presidential term is not possible).

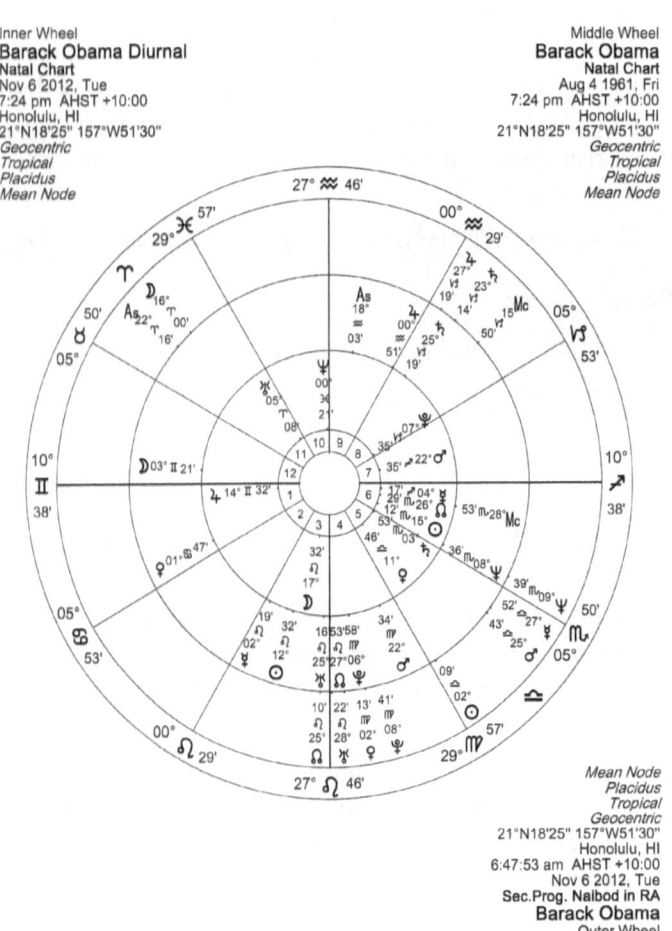

- Progressed Venus will conjunct natal Pluto in the fourth house at about the same time (2016). Time to go home, power intact?

Joe Biden

Joe Biden's diurnal chart is probably the clearest of all:

- Diurnal Ascendant at 23 Scorpio with the diurnal Node in the first house conjunct natal Mercury-Sun-Venus.

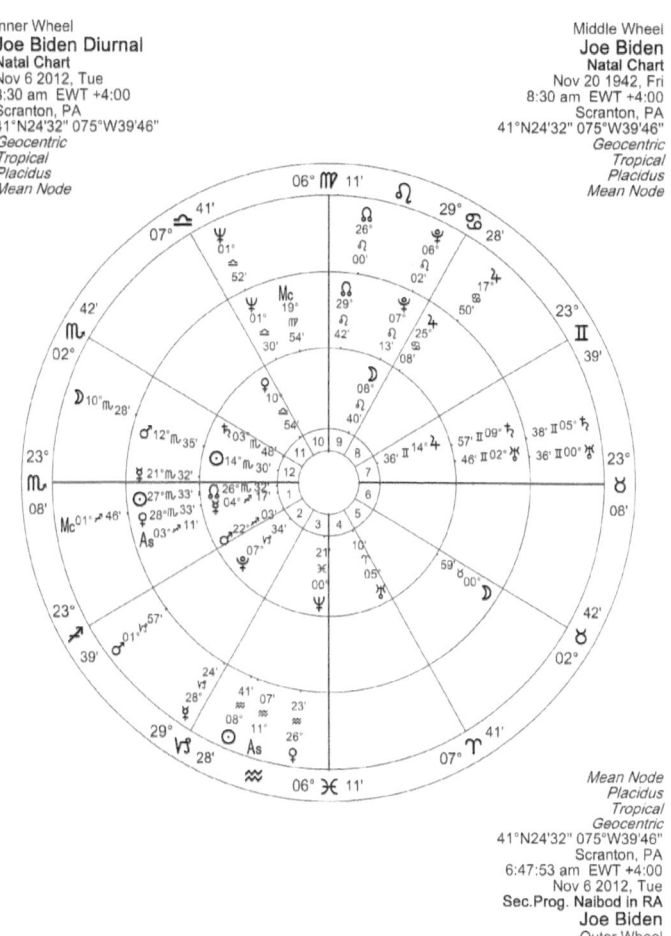

- Diurnal Mercury conjunct the natal Ascendant and progressed Midheaven, all of which are opposition natal and progressed Saturn and Uranus in the diurnal seventh house.
- The diurnal Moon is conjunct natal Pluto (power).
- The Diurnal Sun is conjunct natal Mars and progressed Moon, which I see as a signature of this man.

Astrological Decision Time

There is a lot of activity in these charts, which are more positively tilted to the Obama-Biden ticket; but both presidential candidates have the ruler of the Ascendant in a weak position, with the rulers close to the opponent (Descendant) angle. Do you trust the planet on the angle or the ruler of the angle?

About two weeks prior to the election I settled on the Jupiter rising and the Obama-Biden ticket but wanted more solid proof. Two concepts grabbed my attention:

Rachel Maddow of MSNBC explained how we could end up with Speaker of the House John Boehner as president and Joe Biden as vice president. Talk about scrambling my brain! She was right; such a result is possible. Only two men could take the oath of office. Which pair would it be? I set the inauguration for all five men for January 20, 2013. Three men had to lose as only two men could win the day. We know the results of the election, but this is an autopsy, a forensic search for answers. Let's start with the wild card, John Boehner.

The dates for the election and the inauguration are only about ten weeks apart. The Founding Fathers had chosen March 4 as inauguration day, but a later U.S. Congress changed the date to January 20 in time for F. D. Roosevelt's second term. The angles on the diurnals will shift forward seventy-five days, and the diurnal Moon and faster-moving planets will change by inauguration day. The progressed charts will be relatively unchanged so we will concentrate on the diurnals and the progressed Moon.

If you look strictly at John Boehner's diurnal chart, there are no planets within two to three degrees of the angles; this would be unusual if the election were a key event in his life. (Note: the chart is calculated for noon, November 17, 1949, Cincinnati, Ohio, because the birth time is unavailable; the angles are thus speculative.)

Comparing the natal chart to the diurnal, nothing leaped off

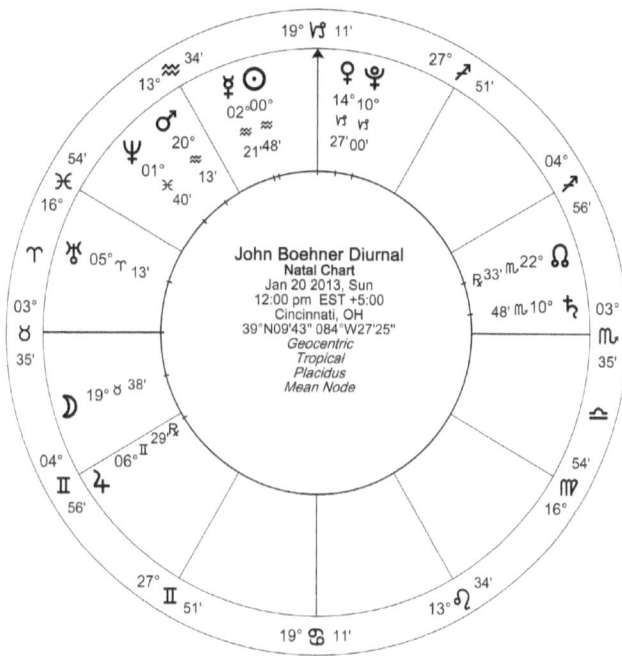

the page. There is a square between the diurnal Midheaven and natal Moon-Neptune conjunction and progressed Neptune.

Interestingly, the progressed angles are very close to the diurnal angles, about two degrees different, but no planets line up with the diurnal angles.

I did not see inauguration for Speaker Boehner.

Romney's diurnal chart for inauguration day has these factors:

- No diurnal planets near the angles.
- Natal Mercury close to the diurnal Ascendant.
- Natal and progressed Uranus close to the diurnal IC.

This chart does not indicate an inauguration.

Ryan's diurnal chart for inauguration day shows only:

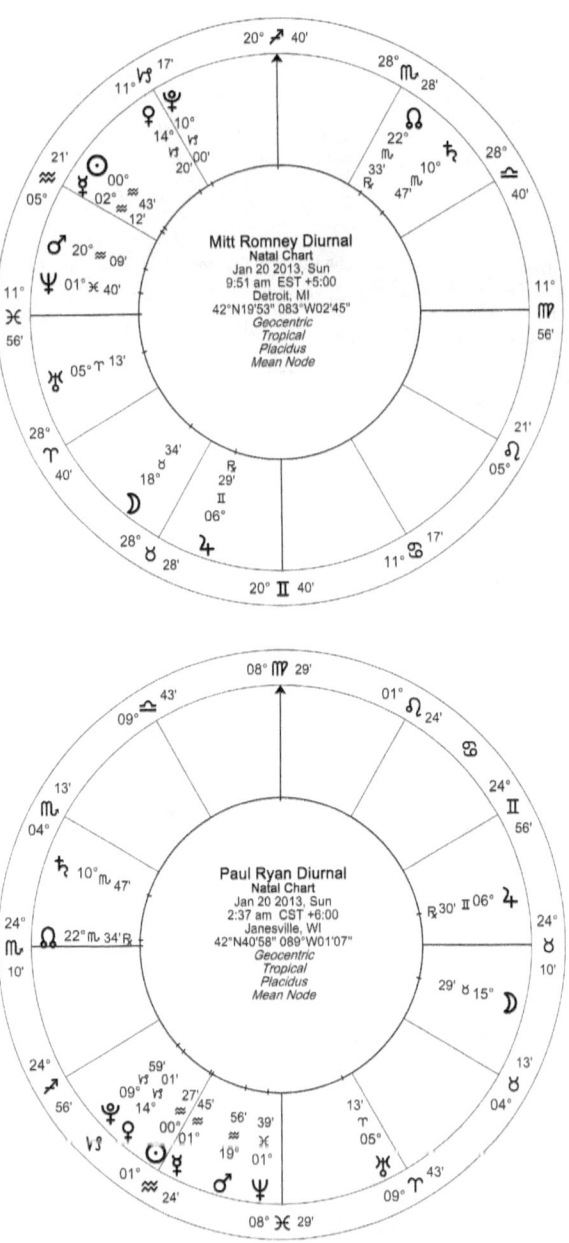

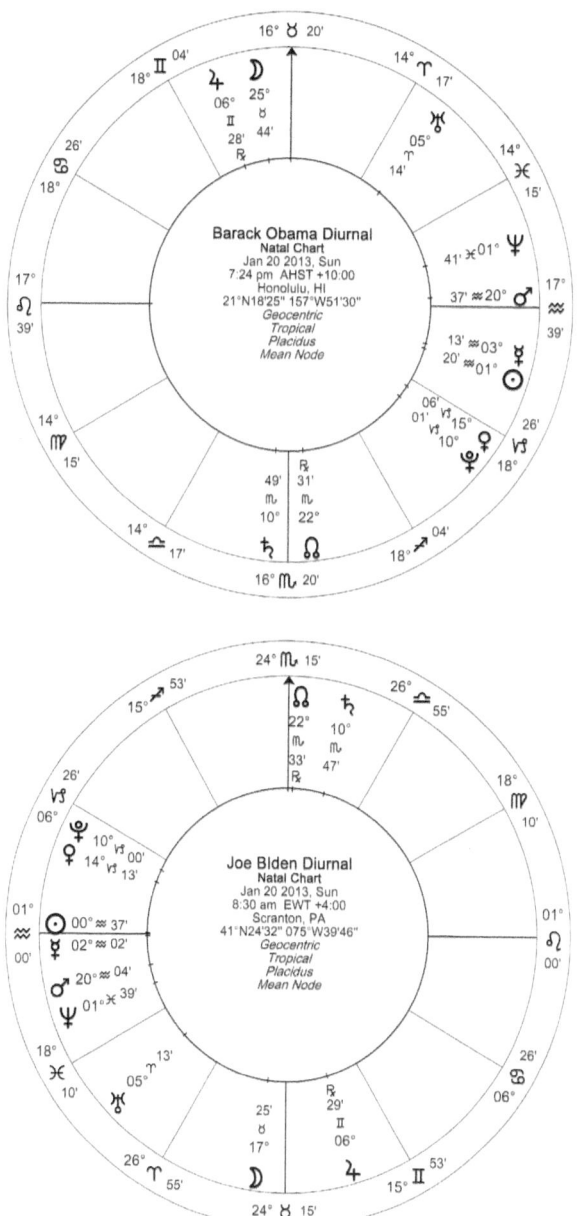

- North Node conjunct the Ascendant with no planets nearby.
- No natal connections to the diurnal chart.
- Progressed South Node conjunct the diurnal Midheaven and progressed Mercury conjunct the diurnal IC within about four degrees.

This chart does not show enough for an inauguration.

I noticed Ryan's diurnal Saturn at about fourteen degrees behind the Ascendant. This is important because the Ascendant moves forward about three-quarters to two degrees per day; so Saturn would be conjunct the diurnal Ascendant in early January. The first week in January is when the congressional members are sworn in. (Ryan ran simultaneously for vice president and for reelection to his congressional seat; he was reelected.)

Obama's diurnal chart for inauguration day shows:

- Mars conjunct the Descendant (about three degrees).
- The natal Ascendant is conjunct the diurnal Descendant.
- The diurnal Moon is conjunct the fixed star Capul Algol (not a good placement, he could "lose his head") conjunct the natal IC.
- The diurnal Sun is conjunct natal Jupiter.
- Diurnal Venus is conjunct the progressed Midheaven.

This chart indicates more of the kind of action necessary for an inauguration.

Biden's diurnal chart for inauguration day shows:

- A diurnal Sun-Mercury-Ascendant conjunction.
- Diurnal North Node-Midheaven is conjunct natal Sun-Venus-Mercury.
- Diurnal Jupiter is conjunct natal Uranus-Descendant-Saturn.
- Progressed Moon is conjunct diurnal Saturn, nearly exact.

Women's Astrology in India

By Ronnie Gale Dreyer, MAFA

In this article, I introduce the genre of *strījātaka* (Sanskrit for "women's astrology") in India, which appears for the first time in a Sanskrit astrological text called *Vrddhayavanajātaka* (Sanskrit for "great or old Greek astrology")—the earliest extant Sanskrit text solely on *jātaka* (Indian horosopy)—written around 300-325 CE by Mīnarāja, an Indian of Greek descent. Mīnarāja's *strījātaka* consisted of five chapters (58-62), that did not utilize sophisticated mathematical models, but used simple placements, such as the position of the Ascendant or Moon in a particular zodiacal sign, to enumerate values to which women in Indian society should aspire. This unique genre, which to our knowledge did not appear in Sanskrit texts or any other astrological literature prior to this time, emerged in India at a time when Greek horoscopy and Indian *naksatra*-based astrology coalesced to form a cohesive system for interpreting horoscopes.

Astrological Research

First, it is important to note a few things about researching Indian astrology in general, and women's astrology in particular. In all of the Sanskrit texts presently available to us, probably the subject most covered is *jyotihśāstra* (Sanskrit for "science of the stars" or "astral sciences"), the branch of learning that includes mathematics, astronomy, divination, and astrology. According to the late David Pingree,[1] as many as 100,000 manuscripts exist worldwide on the various aspects of *jyotihśāstra,* but even more texts, which we know about from references by other scholars have either been lost, or locked away in private collections or remote libraries. This makes it that much more challenging to research a subject like *jyotihśāstra,* let alone a sub-discipline with as narrow a focus as *strījātaka,* especially since much of the available material on women's astrology does not exist as a standalone text, but must be gleaned from other manuscripts, in which they are embedded. Furthermore, most of these have not been translated into English.

Development of Jyotihśāstra

Some background on the origins of Indian astrology in general and natal astrology in particular is essential to understand the place *strījātaka* holds within the development of Indian horoscopy. Prior to the introduction of the zodiac into India, Indians divided the sky into 27 or 28 star clusters (depending on the purpose for which they were listed and used) called *naksatras* or lunar mansions. These fixed star groupings into which the ecliptic was divided were used to demarcate the specific location of the Moon at any given time, rather than just pointing to it in the sky. By dividing the sky into these groups, which often centered around a prominent star within a particular cluster of stars (e.g., Aldebaran, the bright red star, within the *naksatra* of *rohinī*), each cluster, or *naksatra,* was named and located, thus formulating a reference point for the position of the Moon, as well as for the Sun, in order to plan harvesting cycles, perform Vedic rituals, and even plan important events like marriage, or the naming of a child, etc.

Often translated into English as "lunar mansions," the naksatras were used to mark the path of the Moon in its 27.3 day sojourn through the fixed stars along the ecliptic, and are believed to have been established as the basis of the early lunar calendars around 2240-1760 BCE, during which time the vernal (spring) equinox, which began the New Year, occurred in or near the Pleiades whose stars comprise the *naksatra* of *krttikā*.[2]

The earliest actual text was the jyotisa vedanga (jyotisa as a limb of the vedas) written by Lagadha in the first millennium BCE, and represents one of the earliest Indian soli-lunar calendars.[3] This was calculated by observing and recording the cycles of the rising and setting of the Sun and Moon over time; it represents the earliest stage of Indian calendrical tradition, and all the basic elements that characterize the Indian calendar can be found within it.[4] Up until the appearance of the calendar, the word *naksatra* was used synonymously with "star," as well as with "Sun," but with the development of a soli-lunar calendar to time Vedic rituals, the word *naksatra* came to refer to each of the 27 or 28 star groupings, rather than to an individual star. Thus whenever the word *naksatra* is used, it always means the Moon's *naksatra* or, more specifically, the *naksatra* that the Moon is passing through at a particular moment in time.

The Development of Indian Horoscopy

As part of the wave of cultural and scientific innovations that occurred in India during the first and second centuries CE, natal astrology, or jātaka, emerged as a full-fledged mathematical and interpretive system that synthesized Indian naksatra-based astrology with Hellenistic horoscopic techniques. Śārdūlakarnāvadāna,[5] a Buddhist text dating from around the first century CE, is the first extant Sanskrit text that includes chapters on timing of activities to be undertaken, meteorological conditions, and an exhaustive list of all types of omens. Rather than being a definitive astrology text, this information is all revealed by someone who, despite being of a low caste, nonetheless demonstrates his wisdom in the field of astrology, which was considered to only be the domain of high-caste Brahmin priests. Most noteworthy, however, is that the appearance of these stories marks the first time that the position of the Moon's *naksatra* at the moment of birth was used to portend the fate of the individual, even though the description of each *naksatra* as it affects the individual is very succinct and only consists of one or two attributes per *naksatra*.

Since the *naksatras* were formulated as a way of marking off time by using the movement of the Moon through the constellations, it is always understood that when the word *naksatra* is used, it refers only to the Moon's *naksatra*. Thus, if the translation reads "the person born in *krttikā* or *rohinī*," it is understood that it means "the person born when the Moon is in *krttikā* or *rohinī*." The next list of *naksatras* relating to the individual will not appear until two centuries later.

Yavanajātaka

Other than the Śārdūlakarnāvadāna, which only contains one brief section on the fate of the individual, the earliest extant Sanskrit text on genethlialogy is the *Yavanajātaka* (Greek horoscopy), composed in 269/270 CE by Sphujidhvaja, an Indian of Greek descent. This work, which was compiled, translated into English, and completely annotated by Pingree,[6] was an adaptation into meter of an earlier Sanskrit manuscript by Yavaneśvara, another Indian of Greek descent (149/150 CE). That text, according to Pingree, was translated from a Hellenistic astrological text probably written in Egypt toward the beginning of the second century. Unfortunately, neither Yavaneśvara's translation nor the original Hellenistic text has been recovered.[7]

Despite missing fragments of text, Pingree pieced much of it together, transformed *Yavanajātaka* into a readable text that showed how Hellenistic concepts were combined with uniquely Indian ones. Most notable was its introduction of the use of the zodiac[8] as the primary backdrop for the *grahas* (Sanskrit for "seizers," or planets), which in the third century CE amounted to Sun, Moon, Mars, Mercury, Jupiter, Venus, and Saturn. For the first time, the concept of the horoscope was introduced whereby the planets positioned against the backdrop of the *rāśis* (Sanskrit for "heaps" or zodiacal signs) and in relation to one another at the moment of birth, would be interpreted to portend the fate of the individual. The signs were used to categorize everything from dwelling places to body parts to vocation to colors, and chapters of the *Yavanajātaka* included descriptions of what it meant for those categories to have the planets in the signs.

Though much of *Yavanajātaka* was derived from Greek sources, chapters on subjects like Indian flora and fauna, the use of the *nakṣatras* for military strategy, *praśnaśāstra* (Sanskrit for "science of inquiry" or "interrogational astrology"), *muhūrtaśāstra* ("science of the moment" or electional astrology), and other areas of interest originated in India, and may be attributed to the third-century astrologer Satya, whose name was referenced by Sphujidhvaja and later astrologers such as Mīnarāja and Varāhamihira, even though no texts directly attributed to Satya have survived.[9] Still, much of what has become standard Indian astrology has its roots in many of the Hellenistic concepts introduced in this text, as well as these new Indian techniques that were recorded here for the first time.

Vrddhayavanajātaka

As far as we know, the next astrological work did not appear until almost a half century later, and further changed the direction of Indian horoscopy. *Vrddhayavanajātaka* ("Great or Old Greek Horoscopy"),[10] a text on horoscopy comprised of 71 chapters, was composed around 300-325 CE by Mīnarāja, a figure about whom we know very little except that he was an Indian overlord of Greek descent who lived in the late third-early fourth century CE, and likely came from the same social milieu as Sphujidhvaja and Yavaneśvara.[11]

The dating of *Vrddhayavanajātaka* places it in the midst of the fertile intellectual climate of India in the first few centuries CE. From an astrological perspective, it marks the transformation of Indian astrology from a nakṣatra-based system of omens and rituals to a Greek-influenced system that used the horoscope to determine the fate of the individual. *Vrddhayavanajātaka* is almost double the size of *Yavanajātaka* and the bulk of the content of the chapters, numbered 1-57, are similar but not identical to chapters in *Yavanajātaka*. The remaining chapters include: Chapters 58-62, listed under the heading of *Strījātaka*; Chapter 63, covering *nakṣatras* for men; and Chapters 64-71, detailing omens that, according to Pingree, originated with a text called *Garga Saṃhitā*.[12]

With the exception of the chapters on omens, which Pingree believes were added later, *Vṛddhayavanajātaka* is unique in that it is the earliest extant text dedicated solely to horoscopy; there is nothing on military history, horary astrology, or electional astrology, all of which had been included in *Yavanajātaka*. It is also the first time since the *Śārdūlakarṇāvadāna* that the Moon's *nakṣatra* was used for individual prognostication, and from this point forward in all *jātaka* (natal astrology) literature, the Moon's *nakṣatras* would continue to be used in a mundane fashion to time rituals and activities, as well as in natal horoscopes to interpret the individual's destiny.

Furthermore, this is the first time that material on women's astrology appeared, since there does not seem to be any record of Sanskrit texts, extant or otherwise, that include material on women's horoscopy, or even textual references to it, that predate this text in Indian astrological works, or even in Hellenistic astrological works, for that matter. This means that this subject matter either originated with Mīnarāja, or was derived from another, as yet unknown, source.

Strījātaka (Women's Astrology)

The following are descriptions of each of the five chapters that are bundled under the heading of women's astrology in *Vṛddhayavanajātaka:*

- Chapter 58. Description of the 12 Ascendants;
- Chapter 59. Description of the Moon in each of the 12 signs;
- Chapter 60. The qualities of the Moon in each of the 27 *Nakṣatras*;

- Chapter 61. The planets (Sun through Saturn) in each of the 12 houses; and
- Chapter 62. *Raj* (royal) yogas, or "auspicious combinations."

Due to space retrictions, it is impossible to go into a lengthy description but the following sums up the important aspects of each chapter. All translations are my own.

Chapter 58. The 12 Ascendants. In this chapter, Mīnarāja describes in twelve verses the woman's attributes when each of the twelve zodiacal signs constitutes the *lagna* (Sanskrit for "Ascendant"). Each Ascendant alternates between providing negative and positive traits, so that the qualities a woman possesses when her Ascendant is one of the odd-numbered signs—Aries, Gemini, Leo, Libra, Sagittarius, and Aquarius—are inauspicious, while the attributes she possesses when her Ascendant is one of the even-numbered signs—Taurus, Cancer, Virgo, Scorpio, Capricorn, and Pisces—are auspicious. For example

> When Aries rises the woman is not truthful, cruel, always full of anger, excessively phlegmatic, has speech that is cruel, always disaffected from her own relatives.

> When Taurus rises, the woman will be intent on truth, agreeable, have modest conduct and devoted to her husband, skilled in all the 64 arts,[13] attached to her own group, sweet to her husband's words.

> In the Ascendant of Gemini, the woman has very cruel speech, is very lustful, and devoid of virtues, always cruel, full of phlegm and bile, extravagant, and has cruel behavior.

> In the Ascendant of Cancer, the woman is fertile, beautiful, wealth, and good conduct, one who is dear to relatives, has behavior that is noble, resplendent and endowed with proper pleasures.

The reasons for alternating between positive and negative Ascendants in women's astrology lies in Minaraja's description in the very first chapter of odd-numbered signs as cruel or harsh and, as a result, masculine, while even-numbered signs are gentle or kind, thereby more appropriate for a woman to handle. It is also important to note that in early texts there is no categorization according to element and, therefore, it would not be accurate in this context to say that fire and air signs are negative, or earth and water signs are positive; the signs are always categorized according to whether they are odd or even. Since the verses alternate between having negative and positive traits, it is immediately clear which Ascendants will have favorable and unfavorable attributes.

This list of attributes is fairly standard and predictable in terms of what will and will not conform to an idealized Indian society at this time. The positive attributes that a woman will have when her Ascendant is even-numbered include beauty, modesty, devotion to her husband, giving birth to many sons, veracity, being agreeable, attached to righteousness, and skilled in all the 64 arts. The unfavorable qualities that a woman will have when the Ascendant is odd-numbered include, not surprisingly, dishonesty, cruelty, anger, excessive phlegm, sharp speech, argumentative behavior, giving birth to daughters, having low energy, and being emaciated. For the most part, these qualities will be consistently repeated throughout all five chapters.

In Indian horoscopy, the qualities of the Ascendant and the Moon (as shown in Chapter 59,) are most important in defining the woman's destiny. This is because as the sign on the eastern horizon, the Ascendant represents the easternmost point and thus the beginning of the horoscope. The sign that is rising encompasses the entire first house of the chart and the other signs follow sequentially. Thus, if the Ascendant is Taurus, then the first house is comprised of the entire sign of Taurus, the second house is comprised of the entire sign of Gemini, the third house is comprised of the entire sign of Cancer, etc. Today we know this as a whole sign house system, but in the era that this text was written, this system provided the only way that the houses were calculated.

Chapter 59. Qualities of the Moon's Sign. In this chapter, the author describes the attributes of a woman when the Moon occupies each of the 12 signs. Due to the importance of the Moon, and the benefic role that it plays in Indian mythology and astrology, especially as it waxes and enjoys fullness, its position in the zodiacal signs are all mostly favorable. There are a few qualities of the Moon in a particular sign that are unfavorable, but still there is not as much negativity as we saw with particular Ascendants. The following are descriptions of the Moon in Aries through Cancer, as a way of comparing these to the above descriptions of the Ascendants in those same signs.

> The woman born when the Moon is located in Aries will be bold, intent on leading, important, have a beautiful body, is devoted to her husband, always devoted to her elders.

> When the Moon is situated in Taurus, she will be good-tempered, interested in investigating knowledge and attached to the Vedas, fond of sacred places, has many children and grandchildren, and is dear to her husband through her acquisition of wealth.

> When the Moon is situated in Gemini, she will be modest, beautiful, and lovely to look at, have various means of wealth, intelligent, skilled in helping others, has beautiful eyes.

> The woman born when the Moon is located in Cancer will be respected among her own relatives, dignified, will overcome her enemies, devoted to gods and Brahmans.

Although the Moon is not particularly representative of wealth or property in the chart, there are many mentions of money throughout this chapter, more so than when the Ascendant is described. In addition to the above mentions of money in Taurus (is dear to her husband through her acquisition of wealth) and Gemini (has various means of wealth), other mentions of money include: good fortune through her husband (Moon in Leo), much cattle (Moon in Virgo), abundant treasure (Moon in Scorpio), wealth that is connected with her sons (Moon in Aquarius). Although having wealth and property will always be listed as attributes throughout this text, it seemed that it was mentioned more often in this particular chapter.

Chapter 60 on the Qualities of the Moon in each of the 27 Naksatras. In this chapter, there are 27 verses, each of which lists the qualities with which a woman is endowed when the Moon is in a particular *naksatra* at the moment of her birth. This is the first time since the writing of Śardulakarnāvad*āna* two centuries earlier that the *naksatras* were used to analyze the fate of the individual—since they are only used to define military strategies in *Yavanajātaka*—and the only text in which they are listed separately for women and men. As in Chapter 58 on Ascendants, the Moon's placements in the *naksatras* provide both auspicious and inauspicious qualities for the woman, though they do not alternate between odd and even-numbered *naksatras*. In general, the majority of the *naksatras* provide the woman with virtues, good looks, money, and devotion to the husband—the same positive traits that were listed in the other chapters.

Despite this, there still are a few *naksatras*—*bharan*ī, *krttikā*, *āś*lesā, and *mūla*, as well as others—where the Moon's position is not only unfavorable, but completely inauspicious for those who have the misfortune of being born on that day. The *naksatras* that can do harm to an individual are often the same ones that would never be chosen as a day on which to begin fruitful ventures, or get married, and since each *naksatra* is ruled by a deity, and the malevolent ones usually have inauspicious gods and goddesses as their rulers—*bharanī*, for instance, is ruled by Yama, Lord of Death. Some examples of descriptions of *naksatras* are:

When born in *aśvinī* (0 Aries-13 Aries 20) the woman is agreeable, has abundant wealth, and is pleasing to look at, has speech that is pleasant, is patient, pleasing, endowed with purity, attached to gods and elders.

When born in *bharanī* (13 Aries 20-26 Aries 40) the woman will be cruel and argumentative, has wicked thoughts, devoid of wealth, has no luster or glory, constantly in dirty or tattered clothes.

In this text, the *naksatras* are listed for the first time beginning with *aśvinī*, and not *krttikā*, since at the time this was written, the vernal equinox occurred in *aśvinī*. Since Aries was the starting point for both the zodiac and *naksatra* list, this meant zodiac and *naksatras* aligned and marked the merging of Greek horoscopy with Indian astrology.

Chapter 61 on Planets in the Houses. Mīnarāja explains the qualities a woman has when each of the seven planets (Sun, Moon, Mars, Mercury, Jupiter, Venus, and Saturn) is placed in one of the twelve *bhāvas* (Sanskrit for "states of being" and the term used for astrological houses) of the chart. This chapter contains 84 verses, arrived at by multiplying the seven planets by the twelve houses, so that there are seven sections, one for each planet, with twelve verses, one for each house, within each section. It is clear from this text that basic rules of interpretation in Indian astrology that are still used today, were laid down in these early texts. The Sun, for instance, will produce inauspicious results in all the houses, except, for the most part, when it is in the third, sixth, and eleventh. This is a standard rule, that the malefic planets do well in the third, sixth and eleventh *upachaya,* or growth, houses. The Moon will, for the most part, create inauspicious circumstances in the third, sixth, and eighth, much like it does today. In the same way, each planet afflicts or enhances particular houses. The following are examples of the Sun producing positive effects in the third, sixth and eleventh houses, and producing negative effects in the first, second, and fourth houses. For example:

> In the first house, the Sun produces a woman who has excessive pain, always afflicted by unhappiness, cruel nature, thin, ungrateful, fond of food of others, lacking in splendor.
>
> The Sun positioned in the second house produces a woman deprived of food and money, who has cruel speech, missing devotional state, fond of quarrels, hateful, mischievous, and having no friends.
>
> The Sun's position in the third house produces a woman always enjoined with happiness, body that is healthy, very beautiful body and face, and large eyes.
>
> The fourth house Sun always produces a woman who is unhappy, sick, has bad teeth, poverty, and disliked by people.
>
> The sixth house Sun makes the woman eminent or brave, victorious over enemies, a woman of sharpness, calm behavior, fond of doing righteous deeds, attached to dharma, fortunate marriage, beautiful.
>
> The Sun in the eleventh house produces a woman who has gains, who has many children and grandchildren, mastering her senses, skilled in the fine arts, patience, has respect from her relatives.

Chapter 62 on Raj (royal) Yogas, or "Auspicious Combinations." Mīnarāja lists 14 auspicious planetary combinations (*raj yogas*) that, when appearing in the horoscope, will bring the woman a good marriage, often beyond her caste, and frequently termed in Indian horoscopy texts as "marriage to a king." In this sense the term "royal yoga" refers to a combination, or combinations, in a woman's horoscope that will allow her to marry a man of a higher status than herself, perhaps even royalty, though not necessarily. When the term is used to define a man's fate, it refers to a man who can either become a king, or reach a higher status in life.

This chapter is significant since it allows for certain *yogas*, or combinations, in the horoscope, as seen in the verse below, in which a poor woman, or one of a lower social status can improve her status through marriage to a wealthy man, or to a king, and guarantee the type of prosperity that under normal circumstances she would never be able to experience. In that sense, it allows for the possibility of lifting some of the restrictions that one's caste or social status may inflict. Although it appears that these texts are geared towards women of high status, qualities like being obedient, having sons and grandsons, a wealthy husband, and being charitable, are traits to which all women were expected to aspire.

On the other hand, this chapter veers a bit from the others in that it clearly allows for people to rise above the caste into which they are born. When the author says that a woman can become a queen with these combinations, he refers, for the most part, to a woman who is of the Brahman, or highest, priestly caste, though not quite royalty. At the same time, he provides a set of conditions that might allow one to marry into another class, though it is not guaranteed. It is definitely a stretch to label this as social commentary of any kind, but these combinations do provide at least the possibility for anyone of a lower class to go beyond whatever restrictions a woman's caste or social status may present. Of course, as we see, there are several different combinations of planets—some of which are complex—that have to fit your horoscope in order for this to be a possibility, so it is not meant to be a common occurrence. On the other hand, the author does provide 14 verses, which make the options a bit broader.

For the layperson, the techniques and technical language may be difficult to understand, and probably not easy to follow, as they are more complex than in the preceding four chapters, in which simple descriptions were provided that most anyone could follow. This is an example of a verse that is less complex, followed by one that is more complex, in terms of astrological combinations.

> When the full Moon is exalted in the fourth place and is aspected by Jupiter she will become a famous queen who has many children and grandchildren and defeats her enemies.
>
> The Sun in the first house and exalted, the full Moon in the first house, and Mercury in the tenth house makes the woman a queen, important to the king, and gives many children and grandchildren.

Since this was the first time that women's astrology appeared in a text, and the first time that the *naksatras* were used for individuals, it seems almost certain that Chapters 58-62, along with Chapter 63, *naksatras* for men, were probably added after the rest of *Vrddhayavanajātaka*.

Women's Astrology after Mīnarāja

Aside from *Vrddhayavanajātaka*, there do not seem to be any extant astrological texts dating from the fourth and fifth centuries, though we do know of their existence from references in the texts of Varāhamihira (505-587 CE), the great mathematician, astronomer, and astrologer who was likely in attendance at the court in Ujjain. Although Varāhamihira is best known for astronomical and mathematical texts, it is *Brhajjātaka* (Sanskrit for "Great Horoscopy"), which became the classic text on natal astrology, from which all future texts emanated. Most of these subsequent authors copied both Varāhamihira's style and his content, with many passages replicated almost word for word.

Although Varāhamihira adapted many Hellenistic techniques from *Yavanajātaka* and *Vrddhayavanajātaka*, including *strījātaka* material, he "Indianized" the material even further, as well as revising and abridging it. According to Pingree, *Brhajjātaka* was written around 550 CE, and Bhattotpala, an astronomer and author in his own right, wrote its commentary, *Jagaccandrikā*, around 970 CE.[14]

Varāhamihira continued in the tradition of including women's astrology, but its usage and interpretation differed greatly from M*ī*narāja's five chapters, possibly because of how astrology and the roles of women evolved, but more likely, to preserve the brevity of *Brhajjātaka*. Thus, whereas *Vrddhayavanajātaka* consists of 71 chapters, *Brhajjātaka* has 28 chapters. Instead of five chapters that pertain exclusively to women, as in *Vrddhayavanajātaka*, there is only Chapter 24, and the repeated themes are the descriptions of Ascendant and Moon in the 12 zodiacal signs as well as *raj yogas*. Chapters describing the Moon's position in each *naksatra*, and the planets in the signs, are written for men, but in the absence of specific chapters for women, they were and are used to apply to both sexes. Here is the equivalent verse describing the Moon in the first two *naksatra*s, which comprise one verse rather than two separate verses. (Note that *bharanī* is positive here, as opposed to the negative description of it in *Vrddhayavanajātaka*.)

> The person born in *aśvinī* will be fond of ornaments, handsome, popular, skillful and intelligent. One born in *bharanī* will be determined, truthful, healthy, skillful, and happy.[15]

Moving on to the actual material in Chapter 24, *Varāhamihira* tells us in the first verse that most of the teachings are meant for men, except for those things unique to women like the menstrual cycle, weddings, conception, birth of a child, and widowhood. This immediately distinguishes this from Mīnarāja's text in which those things that were unique to women included her eyes, hair and beauty, ability to have sons, and devotion to her husband and community. Mīnarāja's chapters on the zodiacal signs of the Ascendant and the Moon, which amounted to 24 verses, are now simply relegated to the following one verse.

> When Ascendant and Moon are situated in even signs the woman will be feminine in nature, and will be virtuous and endowed with ornaments if they (Ascendant and Moon) are aspected by benefics. When they are odd, she will have masculine characteristics, and will be evil and with no virtues if together with or aspected by malefics.[16]

This verse very succinctly sums up Mīnarāja's Chapters 58 and 59, by still saying that when the Ascendant and Moon are in even-numbered signs, they will be positive for the woman, but in odd-numbered signs, she will be masculine in temperament; Varāhamihira only adds the parameters of whether or not the Ascendant and Moon are aspected by benefics and malefic. While Varāhamihira still places positive attributes when the Ascendant is in even-numbered signs, and negative in odd-numbered signs, the Moon is now also negative in odd-numbered signs, and no longer wholly positive as in the women's astrology of Mīnarāja. This marks the beginning of a standard interpretive factor in Indian astrology, where the Moon and Ascendant are given equal weight in terms of being considered the starting point, or first house, of the horoscope.

Most of the remaining verses in the chapter are concerned with timing of milestones in a woman's life, especially the first menstrual cycle, as that was supposed to explain events of womanhood that would follow. The material includes technical instructions for how to construct and then interpret horoscopes drawn for the first menses, as well as how the planetary alignments in the birth chart provide information on childbearing and on widowhood.

This new type of women's astrology, which provided much shorter explanations than Mīnarāja did and yet included explanations for interpreting horoscopes for the first menses, information on childbearing, and on widowhood, characterized the contents of women's astrology that began to appear as a distinct chapter in most astrology texts that came after *Brhajjātaka*. While the long, though repetitive, descriptions of a woman's values and character that distinguished Mīnarāja's *strījātaka* no longer appeared in the context of classic astrological texts, there was a continuation of standalone texts that came under the title of *Strījātaka*, which synthesized the contents of Mīnarāja and Varāhamihira, though not always with the same combinations. Pingree's list of available manuscripts is an excellent guide to these texts, and there are others in libraries throughout the world.[17] Each manuscript differs in terms of how many chapters are included, and which chapters were included. Most of the time Mīnarāja's five chapters are included, but that is not always the case.[18]

Epilogue

It is clear from my research that there are more questions than answers regarding the origins of women's astrology and the dearth of recorded material. For example, if most of *Vrddhayavanajātaka* came primarily from Hellenistic astrology sources, where did the material on women's astrology originate, since it is obvious that it was written separately. If Mīnarāja originated this astrology, why didn't it appear anywhere else, and were there any connecting texts between the times of Mīnarāja and Varāhamihira that could account for the changes that occurred in both form and content between their works? Other than Mīnarāja's text, there is no trace of that material, except in later texts that anthologize women's astrology by combining the material from both Mīnarāja and Varāhamihira.

Some of the mystery that lies herein may to some extent be due to the actual lack of extant material, or the fact that there never was much material written about the subject. On the other hand, as set forth in the first few pages of this essay, there may simply not be enough interest in women's astrology to inspire a Sanskrit scholar to delve into finding actual or supplemental material that could unravel the mysteries of where women's astrology originated and how it was utilized in ancient and medieval India. On the other hand, it is hoped that renewed interest in classical astrology may lead to discovery of further texts and deeper insight into the genre of women's astrology in early India.

This article was adapted from my MA Thesis and was written with the financial assistance of many generous astrology organizations including Grant Trust, Urania Trust, AFAN, and New York City NCGR.

Endnotes

[1] David Pingree was a professor in the History of Mathematics Department at Brown University from 1971 until his death in 2005, and became its chair in 1986. He is still regarded as the foremost authority on the transmission of texts in the exact sciences from one culture to another. In 2008, Brown University officially closed the department. Many of the thousands of manuscripts he collected now comprise the David Pingree Collection in the John Hay Library at Brown University, with the remainder still in the process of being catalogued.

[2] See Asko Parpola, *Deciphering the Indus Script,* Cambridge: Cambridge University Press, 1994, p 204.

[3] See S. K. Chatterjee and A. K. Chakravarty, "Indian Calendar from Post-Vedic Period to AD 1900," In *History of Astronomy in India*, edited by S.N. Sen and K.S. Sjukla. New Delhi: Indian National Science Academy. 2000, p. 277.

[4] See Michio Yano, "Calendar, Astrology, and Astronomy," MiYano, Michio. 2003. "Calendar, Astrology, and Astronomy." In *The Blackwell Companion to Hinduism,* edited by Gavin Flood. Oxford: Blackwell Publishing Ltd., 2003, p. 377.

[5] See *The Śārdūlakarṇāvadāna.* Edited by Sujitkumar Mukhopadhyaya. Calcutta: Viśva-Bharati Santiniketan, 1954. This edition, though still corrupt in many places, is, I believe, the only available edited compilation. This edition, though still corrupt in many places, is, I believe, the only available edited compilation. "The work was almost unknown to the orthodox Sanskrit Pandits of India. In 1933-38 the celebrated poet, Rabindranath Tagore, the founder of Visva-Bharati, composed one his

best dramas based on the introductory story of the *Śārdūlakarnāvadāna*, one of the oldest Sanskrit works hitherto discovered based on the refutation of the caste-system." Ibid. ix.

[6] *The Yavanajātaka of Sphujidhvaja*. 2 vols. Edited and translated by David Pingree. Cambridge MA: Harvard University Press, 1978.

[7] See *Ibid*, Vol. I. 3. Discovery of a new manuscript of *Yavanajātaka* has led to a reevaluation of these dates. See Bill M. Mak, "The Date and Nature of Sphujidhvaja's *Yavanajātaka* Reconsidered in the Light of Some Newly Discovered Materials," *History of Science in South Asia*, vol. 1 (2013), 1-20.

[8] While it is impossible to determine with absolute certainty when the zodiac and horoscopes emerged in India, we do know that Greek settlers who colonized Northwest India as far back as the time of Alexander the Great's conquests (around 325 BCE) introduced numerous techniques that altered the way Indian astrology would be practiced. We also know that during the first millennium BCE there was trade between India and Babylonia, where the zodiac was actually first developed.

[9] See David Pingree, *From Astral Omens to Astrology from Babylon to Bikaner*, Rome: Istituto Italiano Per L'Africa E L'Oriente, 1997, pp 36-37.

[10] See *Vrddhayavanajātaka of Mīnarāja*. 2 vols. Edited by David Pingree. Baroda: Oriental   Institute. Gaekwad's Oriental Series, vol. 162-163. 1976. Originally planned as a three-volume series, Volumes I and II, which were both published in 1976, contain chapters 1-39 and chapters 40-71, respectively. Pingree had expected to complete Volume III, in which the manuscripts he used for both volumes, along with others he examined, would be fully described and commented on along with "an historical and technical introduction to Mīnarāja's work, editions of some shorter texts related to the *Vrddhayavanajātaka* , and an index of verses." See Ibid. vii. This volume was never completed.

[11] See Pingree, *From Astral Omens to Astrology from Babylon to Bikaner*, 34

[12] David Pingree, *Jyotihśāstra: Astral and Mathematical Literature*. Wiesbaden: Otto Harrassowitz, 1981, p. 71.

¹³The 64 arts are listed in Vātsyāyana's *Kamāsūtra* as a range of accoutrements, so to speak, that a woman should perfect in order to prepare for sexual intercourse. This evolved into a list of artistic and intellectual skills and talents that a well-rounded, upper class woman should possess and range from knowledge of gemology and carpentry to skills in the performing arts to mastery of languages. See Daud Ali, *Courtly Culture and Political Life in Early Medieval India*. Cambridge: Cambridge University Press, 2004, p. 75.

¹⁴See Pingree, *From Astral Omens to Astrology from Babylon to Bikaner*, p. 34.

¹⁵*Brhajjātaka* of Varāhamihira. Translated by B. Suryanarain Rao. Delhi: Motilal Banarsidass Publishers, 1986, p. 396.

¹⁶*Brhajjātaka* of Varāhamihira. Translated by B. Suryanarain Rao. Delhi: Motilal Banarsidass Publishers, 1986, p. 504.

¹⁷See T*he Yavanajātaka* of Sphujidhvaja, Vol. I, 27-28.

***

Ronnie Gale Dreyer is a consultant, lecturer, and teacher practicing in New York City. A pioneer in introducing Indian astrology to Western audiences, she has written articles, reviews, and books including *Vedic Astrology, Venus, and Healing Signs,* which have been translated into several languages. Ronnie holds regular webinars and classes, is on the faculty of ACVA (American College of Vedic astrology), and speaks at conferences around the world. She is NCGR *memberletter* editor, former AFAN secretary and presiding officer, and the recipient of AFAN's Jim Lewis Community Service Award, and the 2002 Marion D. March Regulus Award for Community Service. Ronnie has also been recognized by the Indian Council of Astrological Sciences for her work in promoting Indian astrology. She is NCGR-PAA Level IV certified, and holds an M.A. in South Asian Languages and Culture from Columbia University. Ronnie can be reached at Ronnie@ronniedreyer.com, www.ronniedreyer.com.

Predicting Events

By Chand Karan Ahuja, RMAFA

In today's fast-moving world it has become essential to look deeper into astrology for the occurrence of events over much shorter periods of time than are covered by the Vimshottari or *Ashtottari Dasa* systems of the Hindu Vedic sidereal astrology. For this, the effect of the transiting planets comes in very handy. This is also referred to as *Gocharphal* in nearly all texts that cover the *Dasa* systems and was even recommended by the ancient astrologers and sages of India for determining events over narrower periods of time.

After studying hundreds of horoscopes, I have discovered some truly astounding facts and features of the transiting planets. Having examined these again and again I have found them to be correct. It is therefore my desire to help more astrologers learn them in order to give more precise predictions.

Most of you already know that astrology is an ocean of knowledge. It is the science of all sciences and within it lies all the knowledge of the world. There are many principles upon which the transits of planets operate and it can take a lot of time to even learn the basic principles. However, I shall make a humble attempt to explain some salient features and principles upon which the transiting planets operate and which I have come across in my long tryst with this wonderful subject. Although

I may have missed some significant characteristics in my quest thus far, I would like to share what I have discovered.

It must be understood at the outset that for optimum results the effects and results of the *Dasa* system as propounded by our ancients must be taken into account along with the effect of the transits of planets. First, though, the preliminaries, without which it would be useless to proceed. Below are some of the facts that I have found over the years.

Mars and Saturn

There are two major forces in the heavens: Mars and Saturn. At the time of birth Mars is endowed with a potential in accordance with the strength of its house and sign, and Saturn is hardly endowed with any such potential strength.

Saturn (and what it represents in a natal chart by way of its house and sign) is always envious of the potential and strength of the house and sign of natal Mars and makes an effort to mutate/destroy Mars and build, create, and strengthen the house it is itself placed in at the time of birth. The house occupied by Saturn at the time of birth may or may not be a friendly house. And accordingly the general path of life can be ascertained from this singular fact.

If Mars is in a positive/friendly house and Saturn is not, it can be said that the house of Mars disintegrates/mutates, though gradually, in the lifetime of the person toward a negative end. On the other hand, if it is the other way around then the opposite happens.

A balanced situation can prevail if the disintegration of Mars is from a negative position to a negative position or from a positive position to another positive position.

However, everything is not lost or gained until the positions of other planets in the chart are taken into account. The positions of all other planets are also to be noted for being in a positive or a negative position in the natal chart. For the final result, which will prevail in the twilight years of the person, the position of the Moon in the chart of the person at the time of birth is of utmost significance. If it is placed in a favorable house in the natal chart it can be safely assumed that success would definitely come (ultimately) in the lifetime of the person. The remaining planets also have a role and operate during the lifetime of a person.

There seems to be a general sequence of the planets in which they operate during the lifetime of a person: first Mars; then Saturn; then Jupiter; then *Ketu* (Dragon's Tail) and *Rahu* (Dragon's Head); then Sun, Mercury, and Venus; and finally the Moon.

During their active periods the same values of the *Dasa* system apply broadly and do not vary by more than a year or so. If there are any retrograde or combust planets in this sequence, then the effects of such planets come into play a little later than usual and therefore the previous planet in the sequence has a longer period. This sequence, in addition to the respective houses and signs of the planets, is what has to be noted in the natal chart to get a sort of birds-eye view of the destiny of a person.

The next step is to connect the planets of the natal chart in the order of this sequence with a pen or pencil to obtain a graphical picture of the trend of the planets. From this graphical picture the general success and happiness of a person can be predicted quite accurately. If the graph created by connecting the planets is heading toward the Ascendant, whether it is in the direction of the movement of the planets or not, it can be safely presumed that it will be a fulfilling life. And if it is in the direction of the movement of the planets, then it can be said the person will have a better life than if it was moving against the movement of the planets. However, in case the graph made out is proceeding toward the Descendant, whether it is in the direction of the movement of the planets or not, it can be safely presumed it will not be a very fulfilling life. However, everything is not lost or even gained due to this one factor.

This is just a glimpse into the net result at the end of life. During the intervening period between birth and death there can be periods of joy, happiness, and success, as well as of sorrow, misfortune, and lack of success. These periods can also be determined, roughly, by knowing whether the position of an operating planet is at a crest or trough of the graph of the chart. This applies to all cases of the direction of the graph, whether it is moving toward the Ascendant or Descendant.

Next I will discuss some general characteristics of the planets that are essential before proceeding to predicting the time of events more precisely by the transits of the planets.

The Planets

Mars is an intelligent, confident, and courageous planet (person), bubbling with life and rarely seeking any planet's (person's) assistance to achieve its aims and objectives or even hold on to and protect the house it is situated in from destruction/mutation by Saturn. However, its weakness lies in its short-sightedness, lack of intuition, and hasty action.

Mars is always on the lookout to influence, interfere, and even disrupt the nature or attribute of the houses and signs that are in the fourth or eighth houses from itself, but positively supports and promotes the nature and attributes of the house and sign that is in the seventh house from itself.

Saturn, on the other hand, is just the opposite of Mars. It is not very intelligent but has an ample supply of envy, meanness, and greed. The only feature in its favor is that wherever it is positioned in a chart it has first priority in any situation—and much more so than the other planets. And for countering the features of Mars, it seeks the knowledge as well as help and support of Jupiter; but it rarely gets it and therefore cannot hold on to what it has toiled for and loses it to *Rahu*, *Ketu*, Mars and Jupiter.

Jupiter passes on whatever it has acquired from Saturn to the Sun, the King of the Universe, whom no one dare refuse. *Rahu*, *Ketu*, and Mars hold on to whatever passes onto them from Saturn, all in their respective lunar months.

Ketu and *Rahu* have been generally considered as the mischief-mongers of the entire lot by astrologers. This seems to be a little exaggerated in the case of *Rahu*. But it can be considered to be fairly correct in the case of *Ketu*. Of the two, *Rahu* is passive, yielding, and shy; *Ketu* is active, unyielding, and outspoken. *Ketu* is vengeful and does not forget past injustices. And being endowed with a good memory, *Ketu* strikes when the iron is hot and when least expected by others. It does not yield until it gets its due.

The Sun obtains the knowledge, help, and support of Jupiter to create, support, elevate, and protect the status of the various houses, but especially the seventh house from Jupiter. The transit of the Sun in the seventh house from Jupiter is a very crucial month each year. It usually begins on a sad note but ends positively. It can take a number of days for this Jupiter support to arrive, i.e., until the Moon passes over Jupiter in that lunar month. This effect sometimes begins earlier, from the onset of the solar month. It is in fact the seventh house from transiting Jupiter that stands to gain the most. The other two, the fifth and ninth, which are also aspected by Jupiter, are merely ancillary to the elevation, support, and protection of the seventh house. In Hindu astrology there are fewer aspects of planets than in western astrology. These aspects are listed in a table at the end of this article.

Mercury and Venus always move in close proximity to the Sun. Mercury is never more than twenty-eight degrees away from the Sun in either direction and Venus is never more than forty-eight degrees away from the Sun in either direction. Their roles can be likened to the messenger/servant/minister and queen/wife/consort, respectively, of the Sun. For making important decisions and judicious executive orders (the Sun's duty), it is essential for the Sun to have Mercury and Venus in close proximity for information and advice, respectively. Nature has done exactly that.

Next is the Moon, which represents the mind. Its house and position in transit indicate where the mind of the transiting Sun is occupied and is an aid in determining the exact nature of that house and sign in order to make the right decisions or issue correct orders.

Timing Events

This is quite a lengthy process but very effective and is of assistance in determining the exact date of an event/occurrence. Keeping the shortage of space in mind, I shall broadly explain the method of using it.

After casting the birth chart, the transiting planets should be placed outside the birth chart and alongside the signs they are transiting. Take care to mention the retrograde and combust planets, both in the birth chart and the transiting planets. It is pertinent to point out at this stage that Saturn moves direct and retrograde in a sign. So it would be very appropriate to write the dates and degrees of the Saturn stations outside the chart as well.

Saturn behaves differently with each direct and retrograde period. It is weak in the first direct transit, moderately strong in the second direct transit, and very strong in the third direct transit. In retrograde periods it has no strength in the first, is very weak in the second, and weak to moderately strong in the third.

The basic role of Saturn in a sign and therefore a house it is transiting is to build it. However, its objective may or may not be achieved at all. It depends on whether its house is being aspected by transiting Jupiter or occupied by transiting *Rahu*, *Ketu*, or Mars. It is to be remembered, however, that positivity in these cases will come only during the lunar month of Saturn. Since Saturn remains in a sign for approximately two and one-half years, the house it is transiting goes through many ups and downs. The uptrends come when it is direct and the downtrends come when it is retrograde. In every subsequent direct and retrograde period its strength can be determined accordingly.

When Saturn is retrograde, it is more or less always weak, the matters related to the house it is transiting can totally collapse/ mutate to the house of the transiting Sun and especially so to such houses where *Rahu*, *Ketu*, Mars, and Jupiter are transiting, but only during the respective lunar months of the houses/signs in which they are transiting. Whereas the lunar months of *Rahu*,

Ketu, and Jupiter occur every year, the lunar month of Mars may or may not occur during the course of a year, and sometimes twice if Mars is moving quickly.

Transiting Jupiter is significant in the sense that its house and sign represent the area that transiting Saturn seeks to obtain in order to achieve its ultimate aim of building/creating the house it is transiting; for this purpose its attention always remains fully focused on Jupiter, and especially so when Saturn is retrograde.

In a way it can be said that Jupiter disintegrates/mutates the house of Saturn to the house it is transiting. Since this situation remains for a year or so, Saturn remains bound to the house of transiting Jupiter for that long. Jupiter's most significant role is to pass on what it receives from transiting Saturn to the seventh house from itself.

The transiting Sun, Mercury, and Venus combine (Sun-Combine) to play a very significant role in the timing of events, i.e. of timing of the lunar month during which actual events/occurrences take place. It is during the various lunar months that occur in a year that the Sun and its combine transport/transfer the matters related to the house and sign of Saturn to various houses through which they pass during their respective lunar months.

This feature is better and more easily understood if Saturn is likened to a bucket containing a certain shade/color of paint and the Sun-Combine is likened to that of a paint brush, whereas the Moon is likened to the imagination at play while a picture is being completed of the lunar month. It follows that during a lunar month the picture is hardly conceivable but will be as soon as the next lunar month begins.

Nothing would happen if it were not for the transiting Moon. The Sun, the lord of the universe, would not be able to pass on the traits, characteristics, and all other matters related to the house and sign of transiting Saturn to the various other houses in their respective lunar months if it could not call upon or imagine the nature of all the remaining signs and houses to play their part in thought and/or action. For this, the Sun-Combine taps all the houses with the assistance of the Moon. In all respects the Moon is the messenger of the Sun-Combine.

But the Moon does not spare the Sun-Combine before its influence has flowed from the house and sign of transiting Saturn to the house and sign of the current lunar month. The Moon takes its share of this influence from the Sun-Combine, from the eighth day of the bright-half of the current lunar month and only until the eighth day of the dark-half of the current lunar month. In the process the Moon passes on this influence to the houses and signs it passes through during these fifteen days.

Event/Action Periods

In order to determine when and what event/action will take place, we need to consider the house and sign of transiting Saturn in relation to the periods shown below for 2011:

Aries: July 26-August 20
Taurus: August 21-September 18
Gemini: September 19-October 17
Cancer: October 18-November 12
Leo: November 13-December 6
Virgo: December 7-31
Libra: January 1-30
Scorpio: January 31-March 12
Sagittarius: March 13-April 26
Capricorn: April 27-June 2
Aquarius: June 3-30
Pisces: July 1-25

These periods can begin and end a day earlier or later than mentioned, and will not vary by more than two days earlier or later for other years. During a lunar month, events/actions also occur in the house of the current lunar month.

Quick Method for Finding Events

An event is more significant if it is the lunar month of one of these four planets: *Rahu*, *Ketu*, Mars, or Jupiter, or a combination of two or more of them.

A lunar month has 30 *tithis*, or days. It can begin on any date within a solar month and therefore can last to any date in the next solar month. In any year there are usually twelve lunar months, but there can be thirteen. They are referred to as the lunar months of the sign occupied by the Moon on the first *tithi*, or the first day, after the New Moon. The dates of the beginning and ending of solar months are nearly the same every year, whereas the dates of the beginning and ending of the lunar months vary every year. In each subsequent year the beginning, and therefore the ending, dates of a lunar month begin and end about eleven days earlier than the previous year. To obtain the exact dates of the beginning and ending of a lunar month in any particular year, consult an ephemeris for that year or find them with astrology software.

Once the beginning and ending dates of a lunar month are obtained, determine whether any one or more of the four planets mentioned above are in the same sign as the lunar month. If this is the case, it should be assumed that it will be a lunar month with a significant event or action; otherwise it will be a normal lunar month with expected events or actions.

In order to determine what will happen during a lunar month, take note of these four houses: 1) the house where a new lunar month will begin; 2) the house where the Full Moon will occur; 3) the house Saturn is transiting; and 4) the event house which is/will be active during the period of the lunar month under consideration.

The event house can be determined by first knowing the sign of the period under consideration from the list given and then locating the house in which that sign is placed in the natal chart.

After these four houses have been noted, name them A, B, S, and P, respectively, for the sake of convenience.

The first event will relate to the passing/conversion of matters related to house A, then to house B, and can occur on any date during the period of time the Moon takes to move from house A to house B. The second event will relate to the passing/conversion of matters related to house B, then to house A, and can take

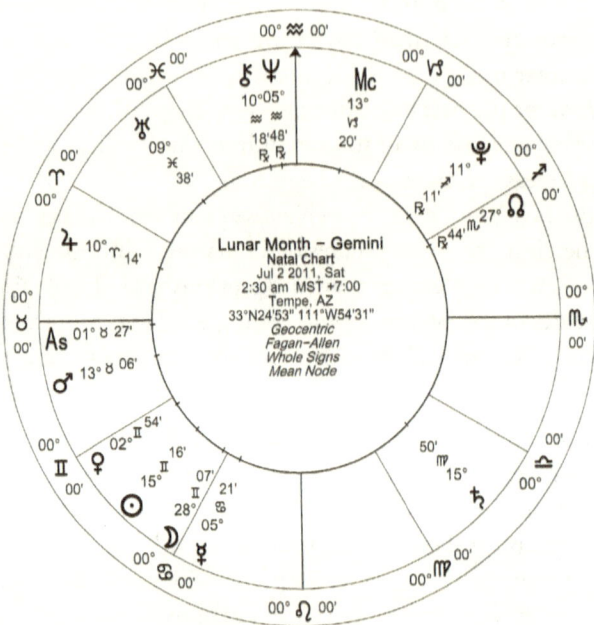

place on any day during the period of time the Moon takes to proceed from house B to house A. House P should not be taken as being related directly to the individual whose chart is being studied but as a house belonging to, pertaining to, or under the influence of house S.

During the transit of Saturn in a house, events will occur directly with respect to the person/matter that the house of transiting Saturn represents and indirectly to the person whose chart is being studied. This can best be explained by an example.

Let us note the position of the transiting planets and the houses A, B, S and P, for the example chart for July 2, 2011, one of the days of the lunar month of Gemini which began on July 1, 2011.

House A is the second house (Gemini), house B is the eighth house (Sagittarius), house S is the fifth house (Virgo), and house P is the eleventh house (Pisces). So during the course of the current lunar month that began on July 1, 2011, and continued until July 30, 2011, the second house (A) first yielded to the eighth house (B), and then the eighth house (B) yielded to the second house (A), for the ultimate benefit or detriment of the eleventh house (P) in relation to or with respect to fifth house (S), which was the house of transiting Saturn in Virgo (the fifth house of the Taurus Ascendant).

During this lunar month an event/action will occur regarding house P, the eleventh house (money, income, job, gains, etc.), so we need to see whether it will be beneficial or detrimental. Since house S, which is the fifth from the Taurus Ascendant, stands for matters related to children, education, official and legal matters, study, research, etc., it could be safely assumed that the eleventh house P was being built/created beneficially with regard to, from, or for the matters related to house S (the fifth house from the Taurus Ascendant). This would imply that income or gains were indicated with regard to, or from, or for house S during the event period. This event period extends until the end of the current lunar month or until the end of the event period of a sign if its duration is more than the current lunar month. Thereafter the next event sign and lunar month take over, and so on.

Planetary Aspects in Vedic Astrology

Planet	Houses Aspected
Sun	Seventh
Moon	Seventh
Mercury	Seventh
Venus	Seventh
Mars	Fourth and Eighth
Jupiter	Fifth, Seventh and Ninth
Saturn	Third, Seventh and Tenth

***

The author can be contacted via the Web site www.astrodesk.com or via email at ck@astrodesk.com.

If done by hand, then bias on the part of the user becomes an issue. The computer has no such bias, and the evaluation of the chart data used is consistent from chart to chart.

As you look at these listings, keep asking yourself questions like "Why is this person (or event) strong (or weak) in the astrological energies of the asteroid Juno?" What is there in the unfolding of time which drew out such energy?

Juno

The top 20 (of 948) people/events strong by all Midpoint Aspects to Juno (N/BY = Name/Birth Year; OCC = Occupation; RR = Rodden Rating; WT = Weight; #H = Number of Hits):

N/BY	OCC	RR	WT	#H
Barbara Hutton (1912)	heir	AA	141.10	165
Pierluigi Martini (1961)	race	AA	122.41	162
Bernadine Dohrn (1942)	terr	AA	114.01	176
Cherrie Moraga (1952)	plwr	AA	113.01	178
Peter Marshall (1902)	reli	AA	108.09	161
Mary Travers (1936)	sing	AA	107.74	169
Friedrich Nietzsche (1844)	phil	B	106.40	165
Maurice McCann (1938)	occa	A	106.40	169
Marcel Proust (1871)	writ	AA	105.01	167
James McLaughlin (1954)	carp	AA	104.96	175
Muhammad Ali (1942)	boxr	AA	104.94	157
Shirley MacLaine (1934)	actr	AA	104.88	154
Henry Cabot Lodge (1902)	poli	A	104.84	147
John Olerud (1968)	bsbl	AA	104.83	183
Carrie Fisher (1956)	actr	AA	104.69	169
Daniel Berrigan (1921)	acti	AA	104.65	158
Clara Barton (1821)	medi	B	104.53	156
Hugh Downs (1921)	talk	AA	104.18	174
Hugh Morgan (1940)	busi	AA	104.05	157
Christa McAuliffe (1948)	astr	A	104.02	162

The bottom ten (of 948) people/events with all midpoint aspects to Juno:

Timothy Mcveigh (1968)	terr	AA	69.93	136
Michel Mollat du Jourdin (1911)	educ	AA	69.85	130
Robin Williams (1951)	accm	AA	68.42	132
Mark McGuire (1963)	bsbl	AA	68.11	127
Johnny Ray (1927)	sing	A	67.67	127
Joyce Carol Oates (1938)	writ	AA	66.35	145
Antonia Fraser (1932)	writ	A	65.79	135
Donald 0'Connor (1925)	acda	AA	65.14	130
Dr. Timothy Leary (1920)	educ	AA	63.66	124
Bob Mulligan (1948)	occa	A	59.83	125

The occupation codes are based on my own interpretation. Some of these people I am not familiar with, so I added the four letter occupation code as a means to help me focus on one aspect of their life thrust. Many of the people have more than one thrust in life, so there is the potential for more than one occupation code assignment. In these cases I simply chose one four letter set that I felt appropriate.

Interpretations for the occupation codes shown above are:

accm = actor/comedian	medi = M.D. (physican)
acda = actor/dancer	occa = astrologer
acti = activist	phil = philosopher
actr = actor/actress	plwr = playwright
astr = astronaut	poli = politician
boxr = boxer	race = race car driver
bsbl = baseball player	reli = religious
busi = business person	sing = singer
carp = carpenter	talk = talk show host
educ = educator	terr = terrorist
heir = heir/heiress	writ = writer

How did I choose the people and/or events for inclusion into the set of 948 data which I used here? Mainly by going through Astrodatabank and looking for a Rodden Rating (RR) of AA or A, and a biographical entry of more than two or three lines. I also tried to extract a balanced set of occupational emphasis. This was not easy as the Astrodatabank data is skewed to famous actors, actresses, performers, and people in general who are considered news-worthy.

Using this Information

You should ask, "How can I use the information presented here?"

Look to how the people or events used the strong or weak asteroid energies as events through time played out with them. I would NOT take the actual weights shown as being indicative of anything, other than these numbers were used to sort who is strong from weak. That is, the top twenty people or events shown above should simply be looked at as "here are some strong Juno chart energies"–and by contrast, the weak Juno chart energies. To reiterate: do NOT use these lists to say or think something like, for example, that Mary Travers has a stronger Juno in her natal chart than Shirley MacLaine. A better way to interpret and use these results would be to think or say "both Mary Travers and Shirley MacLaine have a strong Juno by midpoint in their natal charts."

Where to take this information from here? It is up to you, the reader, to take this information to the next level. Research these people or events to see how they used Juno within and throughout their lives. Does the fact that Barbara Hutton, the Woolworth heiress and actress, has a strong Juno placement by midpoint show up in how she lived her life? Does the fact that Robin Williams, the movie actor, has a weak Juno involvement in his natal chart indicate anything about how he lived his life? Information on the 948 people and events used for this project can be found in Astrodatabank and/or through web searches.

These are the kinds of questions that need to be investigated, and it is up to you, having access to this information, to take this to its next level. The level where real life interactions can help to illuminate the meanings of the asteroid bodies through actual human-time usage. Each reader (or user) doing that can help advance the understanding and interpretation of the asteroid bodies.

Juno Key Ideas

Below are some Juno key ideas gathered and grouped by me from notes taken at various astrology lectures I have attended over years, the writings of authors like Zipporah Dobyns, Demetra George, Lee Lehman, Emma Belle Donath, etc. There is no one source for this information. This is my interpretation of asteroid meanings that others have described. Hopefully these can help you, the reader, focus better on the how the energies of Juno played out in the lives of the people or events noted. You may have additional information or material to go along with these key ideas. The ideas are not listed in any order of importance; all are important.

Union: Upholding traditional marriage and family values. Sustaining, fostering, traditional relationships within a group: like a family, an office, a working team, a theatrical group, a military unit, a business section or division, etc. This includes groups that need to work in harmony. Also one-on-one relationships or inter-relationships like: husband-wife; boss-coworker; a management, sales, or similar team comprised of individuals each carrying equal responsibilities; the cast of a show; etc.

Leadership: Taking the leadership role in developing inter-relationships denoting equality and togetherness within groups, both personal and public, while fostering commitments to such relationships or inter-relationships. Seeking fulfilling unions; yearning for a fulfilling union and/or appreciation from others; working relationships; one-on-one or one-to-group relationships.

Ceremonial Practices: Practices related to marriage or family-types of interactions; the guardian or teacher of such traditional practices; the rites and arrangements of formal ceremonies typifying union; practices designed for including the odd, rejected, or unusual person as an equal member of the group. Sees the value of ceremony or tradition in promoting or upholding group cohesion. Thus not one to "rock the boat" and force changes within groups. The importance of the appearance of ceremony or ceremonial practices. Ceremonies designed to augment position, honor, or self-esteem.

Commitment Within Relationships: Needs for commitment or expectations from or within a relationship; searches for love; what you bring to a relationship, what you take from a relationship; your commitment to making a relationship work; committed partnership.

Anger at Betrayal: when the relationship does not meet your expectations, then any feelings of anger or betrayal generated, or which others cause to be generated, within or by you; timing within relationship events; learning and practicing compromise; fidelity within relationships; attitudes toward one's mate. Concerns for that which we hate or that which we love.

The Feminine: The patroness of married women; the Consort, the Queen; the Feminine Heroine; the Wife; the use of sexuality to transcend personal identity through a committed relationship; a woman's conceiving and child-bearing powers; the role of a wife and/or mate; feminine adornments or beauty aids; the implications of dress and appearance, appearance enhancements; aspiring toward, or showing, the Junoesque figure (i.e., stately, regal).

Planets or Points to Juno by Midpoint Weights

In this section I provide the names for the top twenty strongest midpoint rankings (out of 948 possible selections), and the weakest ten. The "Description" notation provides the midpoint name, degree, and sign pair of location, and the house pair. Midpoints are not a "point" but lie as an axis across the chart. In the sign and house pairings the "head" of the midpoint, which is the closer one, is shown first, before the "tail." That is, the head of the midpoint can be in Aries in the sixth house, but the tail of that midpoint then would be in Libra in the twelfth house.

Sun and Juno Midpoint

Name	OCC	RR	WT	#H
William Shatner (1931)	actr	A	43.540	22
Description: Su/Jn 0:06 Ar-Li 01,07				
Gary Middlecoff (1921)	golf	AA	37.997	19
Description: Su/Jn 2:00 Cp-Ca 10,04				
Muhammad Ali (1942)	boxr	AA	37.811	23
Description: Su/Jn 21:52 Sg-Ge 05,11				
Jayne Mansfield (1933)	actr	AA	37.328	18
Description: Su/Jn 28:20 Ca-Cp 02,08				
Carl Sandberg (1878)	poet	A	36.977	14
Description: Su/Jn 15:38 Cp-Ca 03,09				
Prince Phillip (1921)	king	AA	36.870	20
Description: Su/Jn 29:55 Ps-Vi 02,08				
Bill Moyers (1934)	jour	AA	36.500	20
Description: Su/Jn 24:25 Ps-Vi 01,07				
Bispo Edir Macedo (1945)	reli	AA	36.364	22
Description: Su/Jn 28:32 Ar-Li 01,07				
Marius Petipa (1818)	danc	AA	35.941	18
Description: Su/Jn 9:54 Ar-Li 12,06				
Georgio Armani (1934)	desg	AA	35.754	18
Description: Su/Jn 7:17 Li-Ar 03,09				
Susan Sarandon (1946)	actr	A	35.751	19
Description: Su/Jn 25:12 Li-Ar 09,03				
James MacDonald (1908)	scie	AA	35.458	21
Description: Su/Jn 6:05 Ar-Li 09,03				

Name	OCC	RR	WT	#H
Kathleen McLaughlin (1957)	luck	AA	35.437	19
Description: Su/Jn 29:48 Aq-Le 01,07				
Erwin Rommel (1891)	mili	AA	35.274	19
Description: Su/Jn 8:03 Cp-Ca 12,06				
Joel McCrea (1905)	actr	AA	35.210	19
Description: Su/Jn 29:17 Vi-Ps 10,04				
Hugh Jeffcoat (1934)	gamb	A	35.198	18
Description: Su/Jn 23:28 Ps-Vi 07,01				
Gustav Paul Dore (1832)	arti	AA	35.102	17
Description: Su/Jn 13:02 Sc-Ta 11,05				
WTC Crash (2001)	crsh	A	35.076	19
Description: Su/Jn 22:45 Le-Aq 11,05				
Connie Francis (1937)	sing	AA	35.030	19
Description: Su/Jn 5:50 Sg-Ge 12,06				
Albert Camus (1913)	writ	AA	34.915	17
Description: Su/Jn 13:48 Cp-Ca 04,10				
Friedrich Nietzsche (1844)	phil	B	12.352	8
Description: Su/Jn 18:18 Vi-Ps 09,03				
Robert DeNiro (1943)	actr	A	12.235	9
Description: Su/Jn 4:11 Sc-Ta 05,11				
Randall Woodfield (1950)	serk	AA	12.235	9
Description: Su/Jn 13:15 Sg-Ge 03,09				
Dr. Sam Sheppard (1923)	medi	AA	12.110	8
Description: Su/Jn 25:07 Sc-Ta 12,06				
Steve Martin (1945)	humr	AA	11.414	6
Description: Su/Jn 27:51 Le-Aq 01,07				
Buddy Holly (1936)	musi	A	11.269	7
Description: Su/Jn 6:38 Vi-Ps 08,02				
Sal Mineo (1939)	musi	AA	11.223	8
Description: Su/Jn 16:36 Cp-Ca 01,07				

Name	OCC	RR	WT	#H
Gavin MacLeod (1931)	actr	AA	10.912	6
Description: Su/Jn 13:18 Ps-Vi 04,10				
Alfred Witte (1878)	occa	A	9.481	6
Description: Su/Jn 24:38 Aq-Le 04,10				
Arthur Fiedler (1894)	cond	A	8.707	6
Description: Su/Jn 21:44 Sg-Ge 02,08				

Moon and Juno Midpoint

Name	OCC	RR	WT	#H
Helen Gurley Brown (1922)	writ	AA	41.728	19
Description: Mo/Jn 9:14 Cp-Ca 01,07				
Pierre Balmain (1914)	desg	AA	40.250	22
Description: Mo/Jn 27:36 Ar-Li 10,04				
Steven Spielberg (1946)	dirp	AA	40.071	25
Description: Mo/Jn 20:47 Sc-Ta 05,11				
Gary Middlecoff (1921)	golf	AA	39.520	18
Description: Mo/Jn 18:20 Sg-Ge 09,03				
Nancy Lopez (1957)	golf	AA	39.421	21
Description: Mo/Jn 1:29 Ps-Vi 09,03				
Julienne Mullette (1940)	occa	A	39.228	20
Description: Mo/Jn 9:04 Le-Aq 02,08				
Dick Martin (1922)	humr	AA	38.920	25
Description: Mo/Jn 0:45 Ps-Vi 04,10				
Dave Garroway (1913)	talk	AA	38.712	19
Description: Mo/Jn 25:52 Cp-Ca 04,10				
Vaughn Monroe (1911)	sing	AA	37.991	18
Description: Mo/Jn 23:39 Cp-Ca 10,04				
George Harrison (1943)	musi	A	37.274	20
Description: Mo/Jn 6:26 Sg-Ge 02,08				
Charles Kuralt (1934)	jour	AA	37.254	21
Description: Mo/Jn 17:38 Sc-Ta 07,01				
Eugene McCarthy (1916)	poli	AA	37.058	18
Description: Mo/Jn 8:26 Cp-Ca 11,05				

Name	OCC	RR	WT	#H
Howard Hughes (1905)	busi	A	37.499	19
Description: Me/Jn 19:30 Li-Ar 02,08				
Shari Lewis (1933)	actr	AA	36.829	20
Description: Me/Jn 8:33 Sg-Ge 03,09				
Mary W. Shelley (1797)	writ	AA	36.676	18
Description: Me/Jn 27:32 Vi-Ps 04,10				
Andrew MacTaggart (1888)	engr	AA	36.507	20
Description: Me/Jn 22:20 Ca-Cp 01,07				
R. D. Laing (1927)	medp	AA	36.250	16
Description: Me/Jn 28:50 Vi-Ps 06,12				
Marlon Brando (1924)	actr	AA	35.994	18
Description: Me/Jn 17:54 Ca-Cp 08,02				
John N. Collins (1947)	serk	AA	35.726	21
Description: Me/Jn 7:17 Li-Ar 01,07				
Michael Bennett (1943)	danc	AA	35.576	21
Description: Me/Jn 8:03 Ps-Vi 11,05				
Lee Iacocca (1924)	busi	AA	12.677	8
Description: Me/Jn 25:25 Li-Ar 07,01				
Emily Dickenson (1830)	writ	B	12.184	8
Description: Me/Jn 29:02 Cp-Ca 03,09				
Upton Sinclair (1878)	writ	A	12.152	8
Description: Me/Jn 6:11 Sg-Ge 02,08				
Uri Geller (1946)	occu	A	11.778	8
Description: Me/Jn 7:09 Sg-Ge 02,08				
Carol Lee Newsom (1946)	phot	AA	11.685	8
Description: Me/Jn 3:48 Le-Aq 01,07				
Alfred Witte (1878)	occa	A	11.649	8
Description: Me/Jn 17:03 Aq-Le 04,10				
Mies van Der Rohe (1886)	arch	AA	11.139	6
Description: Me/Jn 28:36 Aq-Le 09,03				

Name	OCC	RR	WT	#H
Ulysses S. Grant (1822)	pres	A	10.894	8
Description: Me/Jn 20:48 Ar-Li 12,06				
Ewan McGregor (1971)	actr	AA	10.822	7
Description: Me/Jn 23:44 Ta-Sc 08,02				
Ralph Edwards (1913)	talk	A	9.887	6
Description: Me/Jn 14:06 Cp-Ca 11,05				

Venus and Juno Midpoint

H. R. Haldeman (1926)	poli	AA	43.251	15
Description: Ve/Jn 29:28 Sg-Ge 04,10				
Edwin Mathews (1931)	bsbl	AA	40.301	21
Description: Ve/Jn 7:32 Vi-Ps 06,12				
Arthur Ford (1897)	meta	B	40.202	21
Description: Ve/Jn 27:09 Ar-Li 01,07				
Rollo May (1909)	medp	AA	38.799	22
Description: Ve/Jn 14:20 Ar-Li 01,07				
Vivian Leigh (1913)	actr	B	38.674	18
Description: Ve/Jn 1:07 cp-Ca 08,02				
Gavin Newsom (1967)	poli	AA	38.573	16
Description: Ve/Jn 20:57 Vi-Ps 12,06				
Louisa May Alcott (1832)	writ	AA	38.455	19
Description: Ve/Jn 6:00 Sg-Ge 03,09				
Noel Coward (1899)	plwr	B	38.206	20
Description: Ve/Jn 16:19 Cp-Ca 03,09				
Leonardo daVinci (1452)	arti	AA	38.179	19
Description: Ve/Jn 5:05 Ge-Sg 06,12				
Liv Ullmann (1938)	actr	C	38.052	23
Description: Ve/Jn 12:17 Sg-Ge 05,11				
Rush Limbaugh (1951)	talk	AA	37.633	18
Description: Ve/Jn 1:41 Cp-Ca 11,05				
J. F. Kennedy Shot (1963)	assa	A	37.522	18
Description: Ve/Jn 29:56 Sc-Ta 09,03				

Name	OCC	RR	WT	#H
John MacLean (1946)	thie	AA	36.888	20
Description: Ve/Jn 24: 4 Sc-Ta 06,12				
Salvatore Luria (1912)	scie	AA	36.708	21
Description: Ve/Jn 20:15 Li-Ar 11,05				
Charles E. Dederich (1913)	busi	AA	36.617	18
Description: Ve/Jn 0:10 Ar-Li 01,07				
Jerry Rubin (1938)	acti	AA	36.445	22
Description: Ve/Jn 14:54 Li-Ar 01,07				
Hugh Morgan (1940)	busi	AA	36.405	16
Description: Ve/Jn 0:54 Le-Aq 10,04				
Ray Bradbury (1920)	writ	AA	36.357	20
Description: Ve/Jn 8:53 Li-Ar 08,02				
Amy Carter (1967)	famf	A	36.208	16
Description: Ve/Jn 25:37 Vi-Ps 03,09				
Jimi Hendrix (1942)	musi	AA	36.187	20
Description: Ve/Jn 9:52 Sg-Ge 12,06				
Joe McGinniss (1942)	writ	AA	12.379	7
Description: Ve/Jn 19:16 Sg-Ge 02,08				
Prince Aly Khan (1911)	weal	AA	12.364	6
Description: Ve/Jn 6:33 Vi-Ps 11,05				
Lance Reventlow (1936)	heir	B	12.320	8
Description: Ve/Jn 25:06 Ps-Vi 11,05				
Israel Regardie (1907)	occu	A	11.919	8
Description: Ve/Jn 6:49 Sg-Ge 01,07				
Burt Reynolds (1936)	actr	AA	11.374	8
Description: Ve/Jn 14:17 Ps-Vi 11,05				
Jack Schwarz (1924)	occu	A	11.075	7
Description: Ve/Jn 12:43 Le-Aq 01,07				
Tornadoes of 1991 (1991)	disa	A	10.945	8
Description: Ve/Jn 7:37 Ar-Li 07,01				

Name	OCC	RR	WT	#H
Alfred Witte (1878)	occa	A	10.386	7
Description: Ve/Jn 17:06 Aq-Le 04,10				
Shari Lewis (1933)	actr	AA	9.521	7
Description: Ve/Jn 3:38 Sg-Ge 02,08				
Prince Charles (1948)	roya	A	8.650	6
Description: Ve/Jn 8:56 Cp-Ca 06,12				

Mars and Juno Midpoint

Name	OCC	RR	WT	#H
Huey Newton (1942)	acti	AA	41.672	22
Description: Ma/Jn 20:36 Aq-Le 04,10				
Michael Bennett (1943)	danc	AA	41.348	23
Description: Ma/Jn 8:32 Aq-Le 10,04				
James Madison (1751)	pres	B	40.860	19
Description: Ma/Jn 11:57 Cp-Ca 02,08				
Sailing of Titanic (1912)	mund	A	40.129	23
Description: Ma/Jn 28:50 Vi-Ps 03,09				
Georges Seurat (1859)	arti	AA	39.855	22
Description: Ma/Jn 15:12 Sc-Ta 02,08				
Arturo Toscanini (1867)	cond	A	38.887	22
Description: Ma/Jn 13:18 Le-Aq 07,01				
Kenneth Greene (1958)	luck	AA	38.317	20
Description: Ma/Jn 8:09 Ps-Vi 08,02				
Eileen McNamara (1952)	writ	AA	38.237	22
Description: Ma/Jn 27:18 Sg-Ge 03,09				
David Wilcock (1973)	meta	AA	38.117	23
Description: Ma/Jn 3:32 Cp-Ca 02,08				
Carl Sandberg (1878)	poet	A	37.994	20
Description: Ma/Jn 0:15 Ps-Vi 05,11				
Douglas MacArthur (1880)	mldr	Re	37.494	21
Description: Ma/Jn 17:12 Ca-Cp 12,06				
Groucho Marx (1890)	accm	A	37.433	22
Description: Ma/Jn 22:04 Sg-Ge 02,08				

Name	OCC	RR	WT	#H
John McEnroe (1959)	tens	B	36.913	20
Description: Ma/Jn 14:14 Le-Aq 10,04				
Mies van der Rohe (1886)	arch	AA	36.723	19
Description: Ma/Jn 6:09 Sc-Ta 05,11				
WTC Crash (2001)	crsh	A	36.571	17
Description: Ma/Jn 14:03 Li-Ar 12,06				
Piers Anthony (1934)	writ	A	36.382	20
Description: Ma/Jn 3:35 Li-Ar 09,03				
Diana Lynn (1926)	actr	AA	36.258	19
Description: Ma/Jn 29:38 Ps-Vi 01,07				
John Nash (1928)	scie	AA	36.060	17
Description: Ma/Jn 0:03 Ca-Cp 12,06				
Dr. Timothy Leary (1920)	educ	AA	36.014	22
Description: Ma/Jn 12:36 Sg-Ge 01,07				
King Ludwig II (1845)	king	AA	35.940	19
Description: Ma/Jn 9:33 Sg-Ge 06,12				
Moina Mathers (1865)	meta	AA	12.592	8
Description: Ma/Jn 12:50 Ar-Li 12,06				
Bill Clinton (1946)	pres	A	11.970	7
Description: Ma/Jn 16:03 Li-Ar 01,07				
Michael McClure (1932)	poet	AA	11.793	7
Description: Ma/Jn 11:48 Vi-Ps 04,10				
Julie Newmar (1933)	actr	AA	11.779	7
Description: Ma/Jn 26:41 Li-Ar 06,12				
William Bonin (1947)	serk	A	11.643	6
Description: Ma/Jn 28:58 Sg-Ge 03,09				
Helen Gurley Brown (1922)	writ	AA	11.511	7
Description: Ma/Jn 12:02 Cp-Ca 01,07				
Introduction of Euro (1998)	mund	A	10.770	6
Description: Ma/Jn 7:05 Sc-Ta 02,08				

Name	OCC	RR	WT	#H
Judith Krantz (1928)	writ	A	10.372	7
Description: Ma/Jn 4:50 Sc-Ta 07,01				
John Ferguson (1948)	serk	AA	10.201	7
Description: Ma/Jn 20:44 Sc-Ta 08,02				
Joe Don Meredith (1938)	ftbl	AA	9.267	6
Description: Ma/Jn 2:53 Ps-Vi 03,09				

Jupiter and Juno Midpoint

Ed Moses (1955)	runr	AA	50.406	17
Description: Ju/Jn 29:25 Vi-Ps 06,12				
Jacques Offenbach (1819)	cmpr	AA	44.771	21
Description: Ju/Jn 29:46 Sc-Ta 06,12				
Woman's Suffrage (1920)	polt	A	43.911	20
Description: Ju/Jn 2:36 Li-Ar 01,07				
J. von Ribbentrop (1893)	mili	AA	41.363	21
Description: Ju/Jn 0:06 Ca-Cp 05,11				
Michael Moriarity (1941)	actr	AA	41.310	23
Description: Ju/Jn 10:03 Ca-Cp 09,03				
Diane Sawyer (1945)	jour	A	41.154	20
Description: Ju/Jn 22:59 Li-Ar 09,03				
Bobby Fischer (1943)	game	B	40.862	19
Description: Ju/Jn 15:48 Ar-Li 10,04				
Jerry Lewis (1926)	actr	AA	39.714	21
Description: Ju/Jn 14:53 Aq-Le 08,02				
Cherrie Moraga (1952)	plwr	AA	39.360	20
Description: Ju/Jn 29:55 Ps-Vi 05,11				
Conrad Moricand (1887)	occu	B	39.314	19
Description: Ju/Jn 19:11 Sg-Ge 04,10				
Therese De Lisieux (1873)	reli	AA	38.726	20
Description: Ju/Jn 23:21 Li-Ar 01,07				
Truman Capote (1924)	writ	B	38.723	20
Description: Ju/Jn 22:22 Sc-Ta 05,11				

Name	OCC	RR	WT	#H
James Earl Carter (1924)	pres	AA	38.336	21
Description: Ju/Jn 22:39 Sc-Ta 02,08				
Joel McCrea (1905)	actr	AA	38.073	19
Description: Ju/Jn 9:57 Ca-Cp 08,02				
Paul Joseph Goebbels (1897)	nazi	AA	38.035	18
Description: Ju/Jn 2:09 Li-Ar 03,09				
Ira Progoff (1921)	medp	A	37.776	19
Description: Ju/Jn 9:14 Sc-Ta 02,08				
Edward Morgan (1938)	lawy	AA	37.534	20
Description: Ju/Jn 15:15 Cp-Ca 08,02				
John S. McCain (1936)	poli	A	37.398	21
Description: Ju/Jn 19:32 Li-Ar 01,07				
Titanic Hits Iceberg (1912)	disa	A	37.339	19
Description: Ju/Jn 20:02 Sg-Ge 12,06				
James McLaughlin (1954)	carp	AA	37.223	19
Description: Ju/Jn 17:42 Vi-Ps 11,05				
Noel Coward (1899)	plwr	B	12.626	7
Description: Ju/Jn 21:59 Sg-Ge 03,09				
Lucky Luciano (1897)	crim	AA	12.296	8
Description: Ju/Jn 8:51 Li-Ar 08,02				
David McGillivray (1954)	runr	AA	11.664	8
Description: Ju/Jn 21:38 Le-Aq 06,12				
Mary Alice Parker (1928)	phar	AA	11.146	6
Description: Ju/Jn 4:32 Ca-Cp 04,10				
Konrad Adenauer (1876)	poli	AA	11.032	7
Description: Ju/Jn 4:00 Sc-Ta 07,01				
Alison Lurie (1926)	educ	AA	10.405	7
Description: Ju/Jn 29:21 Aq-Le 07,01				
Michael McClure (1932)	poet	AA	10.310	6
Description: Ju/Jn 25:25 Vi-Ps 04,10				

Name	OCC	RR	WT	#H
Bispo Edir Macedo (1945)	reli	AA	10.200	7
Description: Ju/Jn 11:30 Le-Aq 05,11				
Tom McLoughlin (1950)	mime	AA	9.778	6
Description: Ju/Jn 18:23 Sg-Ge 08,02				
Rupert Murdoch (1931)	busi	B	9.704	6
Description: Ju/Jn 16:51 Ta-Sc 05,11				

Saturn and Juno Midpoint

Name	OCC	RR	WT	#H
Geneva Clark (1948)	home	AA	43.870	24
Description: Sa/Jn 19:06 Ge-Sg 09,03				
Diane Sawyer (1945)	jour	A	41.894	23
Description: Sa/Jn 7:43 Vi-Ps 08,02				
Jack London (1876)	writ	B	39.505	23
Description: Sa/Jn 19:21 Sg-Ge 07,01				
Carl Sandberg (1878)	poet	A	38.920	20
Description: Sa/Jn 15:34 Aq-Le 04,10				
Mequinho Meching (1952)	game	AA	38.251	21
Description: Sa/Jn 29:50 Sc-Ta 05,11				
C. Morgenstern (1871)	poet	AA	38.206	18
Description: Sa/Jn 22:39 Li-Ar 05,11				
Mac Davis (1942)	musi	AA	37.879	18
Description: Sa/Jn 19:27 Le-Aq 04,10				
Zacarias Moussaoui (1968)	terr	AA	37.862	21
Description: Sa/Jn 25:20 Cp-Ca 02,08				
Jeanne Moreau (1928)	dirp	AA	37.761	20
Description: Sa/Jn 0:48 Sc-Ta 06,12				
Adolph Hitler (1889)	king	AA	37.548	19
Description: Sa/Jn 4:05 Vi-Ps 10,04				
Tammy Faye Bakker (1942)	reli	AA	37.500	20
Description: Sa/Jn 23:08 Le-Aq 08,02				
Manly P. Hall (1901)	occu	DD	37.104	20
Description: Sa/Jn 15:56 Ps-Vi 01,07				

Name	OCC	RR	WT	#H
Patricia Neal (1926)	actr	AA	36.836	17
Description: Sa/Jn 23:17 Sg-Ge 12,06				
James Madison (1751)	pres	B	36.834	22
Description: Sa/Jn 27:48 Sg-Ge 01,07				
Howie Long (1960)	ftbl	AA	36.810	15
Description: Sa/Jn 23:58 Sg-Ge 09,03				
Doris Day (1922)	acsi	AA	36.106	17
Description: Sa/Jn 24:14 Sg-Ge 03,09				
Jean Genet (1910)	writ	C	36.081	18
Description: Sa/Jn 22:51 Ca-Cp 12,06				
Dane Rudhyar (1895)	occa	A	36.056	18
Description: Sa/Jn 12:23 Sg-Ge 12,06				
Steve McQueen (1930)	actr	AA	35.896	19
Description: Sa/Jn 18:18 Cp-Ca 06,12				
John Wayne Gacy (1942)	serk	AA	35.814	20
Description: Sa/Jn 23:30 Le-Aq 08,02				
William Blake (1757)	arti	A	11.337	8
Description: Sa/Jn 2:35 Sg-Ge 05,11				
Robert Matthew (1906)	arch	AA	10.898	9
Description: Sa/Jn 5:13 Cp-Ca 01,07				
Gordon MacRae (1921)	acsi	AA	10.853	7
Description: Sa/Jn 14:15 Sc-Ta 07,01				
Bill Moyers (1934)	jour	AA	10.689	6
Description: Sa/Jn 1:06 Aq-Le 12,06				
John Denver (1943)	sing	AA	10.604	7
Description: Sa/Jn 18:10 Ar-Li 11,05				
1st Atomic Explosion (1945)	scnc	A	10.364	6
Description: Sa/Jn 3:49 Le-Aq 01,07				
Dustin Hoffman (1937)	actr	AA	10.324	6
Description: Sa/Jn 7:25 Cp-Ca 12,06				

Name	OCC	RR	WT	#H
Pierluigi Martini (1961)	race	AA	9.493	6
Description: Sa/Jn 17:26 Aq-Le 06,12				
Vincent Van Gogh (1853)	arti	AA	9.129	6
Description: Sa/Jn 18:57 Ta-Sc 11,05				
Noel Coward (1899)	plwr	B	7.812	5
Description: Sa/Jn 5:57 Cp-Ca 03,09				

Uranus and Juno Midpoint

Robert Redford (1936)	actr	AA	48.849	19
Description: Ur/Jn 29:19 Ge-Sg 03,09				
Judy Garland (1922)	acsi	AA	43.166	20
Description: Ur/Jn 29:56 Ps-Vi 10,04				
Sean Connery (1930)	actr	AA	42.548	24
Description: Ur/Jn 3:30 Ps-Vi 01,07				
Paul Molitor (1956)	bsbl	AA	41.648	21
Description: Ur/Jn 20:38 Li-Ar 04,10				
Philip F. Berrigan (1923)	acti	AA	39.001	21
Description: Ur/Jn 14:57 Sg-Ge 05,11				
Dolly Parton (1946)	ente	AA	38.901	18
Description: Ur/Jn 21:01 Le-Aq 09,03				
Omar Sharif (1932)	actr	B	38.724	19
Description: Ur/Jn 5:15 Ge-Sg 08,02				
Michael Moriarity (1941)	actr	AA	38.310	21
Description: Ur/Jn 10:14 Ca-Cp 09,03				
Richard Mogey (1943)	busi	AA	38.266	19
Description: Ur/Jn 29:08 Ps-Vi 08,02				
Charlton Heston (1923)	actr	AA	37.946	21
Description: Ur/Jn 14:50 Sg-Ge 02,08				
Larry Flynt (1942)	busi	AA	37.824	17
Description: Ur/Jn 3:26 Vi-Ps 04,10				
Babe Ruth (1895)	bsbl	DD	37.711	18
Description: Ur/Jn 12:45 Sg-Ge 06,12				

Name	OCC	RR	WT	#H
Jim McMahon (1959)	ftbl	AA	37.659	19
Description: Ur/Jn 20:16 Vi-Ps 08,02				
Neil Diamond (1941)	sing	AA	37.652	20
Description: Ur/Jn 13:41 Ca-Cp 09,03				
Cherrie Moraga (1952)	plwr	AA	37.462	20
Description: Ur/Jn 28:42 Ar-Li 06,12				
Mark Spitz (1950)	swim	AA	37.391	18
Description: Ur/Jn 17:14 Le-Aq 12,06				
Hank Williams (1923)	sing	AA	37.182	19
Description: Ur/Jn 11:29 Ge-Sg 11,05				
Yehudi Menuhin (1916)	musi	B	36.887	19
Description: Ur/Jn 9:38 Cp-Ca 01,07				
Nancy Kerrigan (1969)	skat	AA	36.005	20
Description: Ur/Jn 21:21 Sc-Ta 08, 02				
H. R. Haldeman (1926)	poli	AA	36.002	21
Description: Ur/Jn 14:02 Ps-Vi 06,12				
Dave Brubeck (1920)	musi	AA	12.197	8
Description: Ur/Jn 19:53 Cp-Ca 07,01				
Ursula Andress (1936)	actr	C	12.174	9
Description: Ur/Jn 16:33 Ta-Sc 11,05				
Oprah Winfrey (1954)	entr	A	12.021	7
Description: Ur/Jn 6:07 Le-Aq 08,02				
Tim McCarver (1941)	bsbl	AA	11.583	7
Description: Ur/Jn 8:24 Le-Aq 11,05				
Bob Hope (1903)	accm	C	11.503	9
Description: Ur/Jn 11:14 Sg-Ge 02,08				
Paul Cezanne (1839)	arti	AA	11.189	7
Description: Ur/Jn 21:36 Aq-Le 04,10				
Ira Progoff (1921)	medp	A	10.566	7
Description: Ur/Jn 4:15 Aq-Le 05,11				

Name	OCC	RR	WT	#H
Carlos Santana (1947)	sing	AA	10.486	6
Description: Ur/Jn 20:57 Vi-Ps 05,11				
Michael Bennett (1943)	danc	AA	10.223	6
Description: Ur/Jn 27:56 Ps-Vi 12,06				
Arthur Janov (1924)	psyc	AA	9.591	6
Description: Ur/Jn 4:16 cp-Ca 09,03				

Neptune and Juno Midpoint

Name	OCC	RR	WT	#H
Stephen Foster (1826)	cmpr	AA	44.012	24
Description: Ne/Jn 2:41 Ps-Vi 05,11				
Ira Progoff (1921)	medp	A	42.678	22
Description: Ne/Jn 21:32 Li-Ar 01,07				
Henry Miller (1891)	writ	A	42.327	21
Description: Ne/Jn 22:29 Ar-Li 01,07				
Maurice Mccann (1938)	occa	A	39.832	20
Description: Ne/Jn 15:06 Sc-Ta 02,08				
Albert Speer (1905)	arch	AA	39.760	20
Description: Ne/Jn 23:47 Ta-Sc 11,05				
H. Ross Perot (1930)	busi	AA	38.837	18
Description: Ne/Jn 17:47 Sc-Ta 05,11				
Robert Motherwell (1915)	arti	AA	38.793	18
Description: Ne/Jn 26:38 Le-Aq 11,05				
Oscar Levant (1906)	humr	AA	38.680	21
Description: Ne/Jn 8:39 Vi-Ps 12,06				
Mitch Gaylord (1961)	spor	AA	38.621	17
Description: Ne/Jn 29:33 Sg-Ge 06,12				
Prince Andrew (1960)	poli	AA	38.528	21
Description: Ne/Jn 29:34 Sc-Ta 04,10				
Gay Gaer Luce (1930)	medp	AA	37.995	20
Description: Ne/Jn 13:23 Sc-Ta 12,06				
Otto Meissner (1880)	lawy	AA	37.908	19
Description: Ne/Jn 5:53 Ca-Cp 07,01				

Name	OCC	RR	WT	#H
Norris McWhirter (1925)	jour	AA	37.873	19
Description: Ne/Jn 13:36 Li-Ar 08,02				
Bela Lugosi (1882)	actr	A	37.243	18
Description: Ne/Jn 20:41 Ps-Vi 01,07				
Sharon Tate (1943)	homv	AA	37.161	21
Description: Ne/Jn 17:14 Sc-Ta 05,11				
Jawaharlal Nehru (1889)	amba	A	36.773	19
Description: Ne/Jn 22:23 Le-Aq 12,06				
Walter Miller (1923)	writ	AA	36.685	20
Description: Ne/Jn 2:25 Ca-Cp 04,10				
Ed McMahon (1923)	talk	B	36.595	18
Description: Ne/Jn 10:04 Ca-Cp 12,06				
Dorothy Parker (1893)	writ	B	36.402	20
Description: Ne/Jn 4:45 Le-Aq 04,10				
Urbain Leverrier (1811)	scie	AA	36.394	17
Description: Ne/Jn 26:26 Sc-Ta 06,12				
James T. McHugh (1932)	reli	AA	13.330	6
Description: Ne/Jn 13:41 Le-Aq 08,02				
Grace Slick (1939)	sing	AA	13.235	10
Description: Ne/Jn 8:08 Sg-Ge 01,07				
Craig Myers (1949)	engr	AA	13.181	9
Description: Ne/Jn 8:03 Li-Ar 06,12				
R. D. Laing (1927)	medp	AA	12.613	8
Description: Ne/Jn 25:03 Le-Aq 06,12				
Ignacio S. Mejias (1891)	bulf	AA	12.329	7
Description: Ne/Jn 18:29 Ar-Li 04,10				
Fred Astaire (1899)	danc	AA	12.088	8
Description: Ne/Jn 25:59 Ps-Vi 03,09				
Eddy Merckx (1945)	spor	AA	11.690	8
Description: Ne/Jn 6:35 Vi-Ps 01,07				

Name	OCC	RR	WT	#H
John McEnroe (1959)	tens	B	11.634	7
Description: Ne/Jn 1:18 Sc-Ta 01,07				
Prince Aly Khan (1911)	weal	AA	11.127	7
Description: Ne/Jn 29:02 Le-Aq 11,05				
Emily Dickenson (1830)	writ	B	9.833	6
Description: Ne/Jn 13:59 Aq-Le 03,09				

Pluto and Juno Midpoint

Name	OCC	RR	WT	#H
Omar Sharif (1932)	actr	B	48.875	22
Description: Pl/Jn 20:32 Ca-Cp 10,04				
Pierluigi Martini (1961)	race	AA	45.157	18
Description: Pl/Jn 5:27 Sg-Ge 04,10				
Gianni Agnelli (1921)	busi	AA	43.490	22
Description: Pl/Jn 6:54 Ar-Li 03,09				
Barbara Hutton (1912)	heir	AA	43.176	15
Description: Pl/Jn 0:12 Ar-Li 12,06				
Gordon MacRae (1921)	acsi	AA	39.887	18
Description: Pl/Jn 6:56 Ar-Li 12,06				
David McGillivray (1954)	runr	AA	38.670	23
Description: Pl/Jn 9:04 Vi-Ps 06,12				
Henry Miller (1891)	writ	A	38.290	20
Description: Pl/Jn 22:42 Ar-Li 01,07				
George W. Lippert (1849)	othr	A	37.956	21
Description: Pl/Jn 8:27 Ge-Sg 07,01				
Brian De Palma (1940)	dirp	AA	37.731	17
Description: Pl/Jn 3:24 Le-Aq 05,11				
Jane Russell (1921)	actr	AA	37.545	18
Description: Pl/Jn 8:14 Ar-Li 09,03				
Titanic Hits Iceberg (1912)	disa	A	37.460	19
Description: Pl/Jn 26:05 Vi-Ps 08,02				
Antonia Fraser (1932)	writ	A	36.928	20
Description: Pl/Jn 18:35 Le-Aq 02,08				

Name	OCC	RR	WT	#H
Patricia Neal (1926)	actr	AA	36.944	18
Description: No/Jn 23:49 Li-Ar 10,04				
Columbia Explosion (2003)	disa	A	36.869	19
Description: No/Jn 26:53 Le-Aq 07,01				
Marc Edmund Jones (1888)	occa	A	36.772	17
Description: No/Jn 17:43 Le-Aq 10,04				
Gustav Paul Dore (1832)	arti	AA	36.232	21
Description: No/Jn 26:50 Le-Aq 08,02				
Rossano Brazzi (1916)	sing	AA	36.209	21
Description: No/Jn 27:04 Sg-Ge 04,10				
Carrie Fisher (1956)	actr	AA	36.189	17
Description: No/Jn 21:44 Sg-Ge 11,05				
Van Cliburn (1934)	musi	AA	35.906	19
Description: No/Jn 18:08 Cp-Ca 04,10				
Josepha Mendels (1902)	educ	AA	35.653	21
Description: No/Jn 14:23 Li-Ar 12,06				
Mae West (1892)	actr	A	12.301	8
Description: No/Jn 15:00 Ge-Sg 01,07				
Mario Andretti (1940)	race	A	12.122	7
Description: No/Jn 15:53 Cp-Ca 12,06				
Yul Brynner (1920)	actr	A	12.065	6
Description: No/Jn 5:03 Sc-Ta 04,10				
Anita O'Day (1919)	sing	AA	11.831	8
Description: No/Jn 2:09 Sc-Ta 12,06				
Vittorio De Sica (1901)	busi	AA	11.819	8
Description: No/Jn 19:59 Vi-Ps 12,06				
Bhagwan Rajneesh (1931)	guru	A	11.509	8
Description: No/Jn 28:02 Ta-Sc 12,06				
Ross Lockridge (1914)	writ	AA	10.301	6
Description: No/Jn 21:41 Ar-Li 12,06				

Name	OCC	RR	WT	#H
Tony Martin (1913)	acsi	AA	8.846	4
Description: No/Jn 22:03 Ps-Vi 07,01				
Ed McMahon (1923)	talk	B	8.556	5
Description: No/Jn 27:20 Ca-Cp 12,06				
Albert Speer (1905)	arch	AA	8.430	5
Description: No/Jn 25:44 Ge-Sg 12,06				

Ascendant and Juno Midpoint

Name	OCC	RR	WT	#H
Pierluigi Martini (1961)	race	AA	46.360	19
Description: AS/Jn 5:30 Sg-Ge 04,10				
Odetta (1930)	sing	AA	41.448	22
Description: AS/Jn 20:01 Aq-Le 01,07				
Joe McGinniss (1942)	writ	AA	40.715	21
Description: AS/Jn 1:38 Sg-Ge 01,07				
Graham Nash (1942)	musi	A	39.228	19
Description: AS/Jn 12:06 Sc-Ta 01,07				
Albert Schweitzer (1875)	scie	AA	39.013	19
Description: AS/Jn 28:59 Ca-Cp 10,04				
Matthew Manning (1955)	psyc	A	38.420	20
Description: AS/Jn 24:45 Sc-Ta 11,05				
George Harrison (1943)	musi	A	37.916	20
Description: AS/Jn 6:23 Sg-Ge 02,08				
Marilyn Monroe (1926)	actr	AA	37.913	21
Description: AS/Jn 26:08 Ta-Sc 10,04				
Burgess Meredith (1907)	dirp	AA	37.579	22
Description: AS/Jn 2:42 Sc-Ta 02,08				
Sir Alec Guinness (1914)	actr	C	36.962	20
Description: AS/Jn 29:56 Ar-Li 01,07				
Carmen Miranda (1909)	acsi	AA	36.858	20
Description: AS/Jn 13:14 Ta-Sc 10,04				
Sophia Loren (1934)	actr	AA	36.857	17
Description: AS/Jn 0:27 Cp-Ca 12,06				

Name	OCC	RR	WT	#H
Vincent Van Gogh (1853)	arti	AA	36.687	18
Description: AS/Jn 21:33 Ge-Sg 12,06				
Stephen E. Nichols (1951)	actr	AA	36.632	20
Description: AS/Jn 15:16 Li-Ar 03,09				
Pietro Mennea (1952)	runr	AA	36.508	18
Description: AS/Jn 23:47 Aq-Le 01,07				
Steven Spielberg (1946)	dirp	AA	35.865	19
Description: AS/Jn 22:46 Vi-Ps 04,10				
Jeanne Moreau (1928)	dirp	AA	35.741	19
Description: AS/Jn 15:11 Ca-Cp 03,09				
Alanis Morissette (1974)	cmpr	A	35.630	20
Description: AS/Jn 23:52 Ta-Sc 10,04				
J. P. MacGillivray (1856)	arti	AA	35.420	17
Description: AS/Jn 5:35 Cp-Ca 02,08				
Auguste Rodin (1840)	arti	B	35.264	18
Description: AS/Jn 22:41 Sc-Ta 09,03				
Charles E.O. Carter (1887)	occa	A	12.686	7
Description: AS/Jn 13:32 Sg-Ge 02,08				
Queen Elizabeth II (1926)	king	AA	12.677	8
Description: AS/Jn 9:03 Aq-Le 01,07				
River Phoenix (1970)	actr	AA	12.676	9
Description: AS/Jn 12:30 Le-Aq 09,03				
Mimi Donner Levine (1927)	occa	A	12.288	9
Description: AS/Jn 21:02 Aq-Le 02,08				
Alice Cooper (1948)	musi	AA	11.813	7
Description: AS/Jn 9:35 Sg-Ge 03,09				
Wayne Newton (1942)	ente	A	11.583	7
Description: AS/Jn 18:37 Aq-Le 10,04				
Germaine Greer (1939)	writ	A	11.270	7
Description: AS/Jn 2:05 Aq-Le 12,06				

Name	OCC	RR	WT	#H
Claude Debussy (1862)	cmpr	AA	11.016	8
Description: AS/Jn 25:59 Le-Aq 01,07				
Bill Clinton (1946)	pres	A	9.708	6
Description: AS/Jn 15:38 Li-Ar 01,07				
Rex Hall (1912)	scie	A	5.598	4
Description: AS/Jn 28:47 Aq-Le 11,05				

Midheaven and Juno Midpoint

Barbara Hutton (1912)	heir	AA	50.694	19
Description: MC/Jn 0:42 Cp-Ca 10,04				
Judy Garland (1922)	acsi	AA	41.915	19
Description: MC/Jn 29:45 Ps-Vi 10,04				
Lord Mountbatten (1900)	poli	B	41.149	18
Description: MC/Jn 2:00 Ar-Li 09,03				
Marlon Brando (1924)	actr	AA	39.541	20
Description: MC/Jn 29:33 Vi-Ps 10,04				
Olivia Newton-John (1948)	sing	A	38.754	19
Description: MC/Jn 15:02 Ta-Sc 08,02				
Ringo Starr (1940)	musi	A	38.574	16
Description: MC/Jn 27:20 Ps-Vi 01,07				
Rob Mariano (1975)	actr	AA	38.430	21
Description: MC/Jn 19:06 Ge-Sg 12,06				
Evangeline Adams (1868)	occa	DD	38.309	24
Description: MC/Jn 11:24 Sg-Ge 09,03				
Willy Messerschmidt (1898)	engr	AA	37.607	21
Description: MC/Jn 13:56 ca-Cp 12,06				
Benito Mussolini (1883)	king	AA	37.003	19
Description: MC/Jn 21:39 Ca-Cp 08,02				
Louise Bogan (1897)	poet	B	36.991	23
Description: MC/Jn 2:26 Sc-Ta 07,01				
Paul Molitor (1956)	bsbl	AA	36.723	17
Description: MC/Jn 28:24 Aq-Le 08,02				

Name	OCC	RR	WT	#H
Steve Wozniak (1950)	busi	AA	36.539	18
Description: MC/Jn 17:57 Le-Aq 11,05				
Jimi Hendrix (1942)	musi	AA	36.237	23
Description: MC/Jn 18:11 Sc-Ta 10,04				
C. Mackintosh (1946)	dirp	AA	35.864	20
Description: MC/Jn 4:31 Vi-Ps 11,05				
Woman's Suffrage (1920)	polt	A	35.419	18
Description: MC/Jn 3:48 Vi-Ps 11,05				
Kent State Shootings (1970)	polt	A	35.323	19
Description: MC/Jn 15: 02 Ar-Li 09,03				
George B. McClellan (1826)	mldr	AA	35.241	19
Description: MC/Jn 24: 35 Ta-Sc 09, 03				
Gavin MacLeod (1931)	actr	AA	35.164	18
Description: MC/Jn 14: 56 Ge-Sg 07,01				
Susan Oliver (1932)	actr	AA	35.131	21
Description: MC/Jn 6:30 Ge-Sg 10,04				
Challenger Disaster (1986)	disa	A	12.114	6
Description: MC/Jn 0:54 Cp-Ca 08,02				
Art Linkletter (1912)	talk	C	12.109	7
Description: MC/Jn 7:15 Aq-Le 07,01				
Van Cliburn (1934)	musi	AA	11.555	8
Description: MC/Jn 3:43 Li-Ar 12,06				
Konrad Adenauer (1876)	poli	AA	11.541	7
Description: MC/Jn 17:53 Sc-Ta 08,02				
Jeff Mayo (1921)	occa	A	11.386	7
Description: MC/Jn 23:23 Li-Ar 12,06				
Winston Churchill (1874)	poli	B	11.287	8
Description: MC/Jn 4:28 Ge-Sg 09,03				
Theodore Bundy (1946)	serk	AA	11.125	7
Description: MC/Jn 21:35 Aq-Le 06,12				

Name	OCC	RR	WT	#H
Dean Martin (1917)	acsi	AA	11.102	8
Description: MC/Jn 19:03 Cp-Ca 11,05				
Mark McGuire (1963)	bsbl	AA	10.525	7
Description: MC/Jn 4:04 Vi-Ps 11,05				
Shirley MacLaine (1934)	actr	AA	6.455	5
Description: MC/Jn 3:30 Ar-Li 07,01				

This article presents much potential for research into the lives of famous people and significant events. It is up to you to take what is here and then use these lists to increase your own understanding of how Juno is and has been used in the lives of these people or the unfolding of the events. Your reading of this article is just the first step in an ongoing and unfolding task in enhancing your education for better understanding of the individual asteroid meanings.

***

Michael Munkasey is a member of the Asteroid SIG, and this article was first published in that group's newsletter. He has also written other related articles for the same newsletter.

www.ingramcontent.com/pod-product-compliance
Lightning Source LLC
Chambersburg PA
CBHW020936230426
43666CB00008B/1696